IN MY LIFE

A double cassette/CD is now available of the Andy Peebles
BBC interview with John Lennon and Yoko Ono recorded on
6 December 1980. Entitled *John and Yoko: The Interview*,
its catalogue numbers are:

Cassette: ZBBC 1196/ISBN 0 563 41153 8
CD: BBCCD 6002

IN MY LIFE

John Lennon Remembered

KEVIN HOWLETT & MARK LEWISOHN

BBC BOOKS

TO PRUE, HUGH AND OLIVER
KH

TO TARJA AND OLIVER
ML

Published by BBC Books
a division of BBC Enterprises Limited,
Woodlands, 80 Wood Lane, London W12 0TT
First published 1990
© Kevin Howlett and Mark Lewisohn 1990
ISBN 0 563 36105 0
Set in Bodoni by Butler & Tanner Ltd,
Frome and London
Printed and bound in Great Britain by
Butler & Tanner Ltd, Frome and London
Cover printed by Clays Ltd, St Ives Plc

CONTENTS

ACKNOWLEDGEMENTS

Sincere thanks to the following for donating their precious time to share with us their opinions and recollections of John Lennon:

Julia Baird, Jack Douglas, Geoff Emerick, Bill Harry, Nicky Hopkins, Jimmy Iovine, Mick Jagger, Vivian Janov, Tony King, Allen Klein, Sean Lennon, Yoko Ono Lennon, Michael Lindsay-Hogg, Paul McCartney, George Martin, Elliot Mintz, Harry Nilsson, May Pang, David Peel, Richard Perry, Keith Richards, Victor Spinetti, Pauline Sutcliffe, Jon Wiener, and our thanks to everyone who helped in arranging these interviews.

For assisting in the radio and book production our grateful thanks to:

Johnny Beerling, Tim Blackmore, Nicky Campbell, Julian Flanders, Alan Freeman, Stuart Grundy, Bill Hamilton, Bob Harris, Mike Heatley, Heather Holden-Brown, Joanne King, Allan Kozinn, Phil Lawton, Roger Lewis, Amanda McGeever, Judy Martin, Simon Mayo, Andy Peebles, Stephen Peeples, PK Roberts, Brian Thompson, John Walters, and the invaluable BBC archives.

The authors and publisher have made every effort to contact those people interviewed and quoted within this book and apologise for any oversight which may have been made.

PICTURE CREDITS

Page 9 Apple Corps Ltd; p 11t & b Tom Hanley; p 15t Rex Features, b Richard DiLello/Camera Press; p 17 Scope Features; p 21t Charles Roberts, bl Pictorial Press/Keese, br Popperfoto; p 25t & b Pictorial Press; p 27 Barry Plummer; p 31 Apple; p 33t Ronald Grant Archive, b Tom Hanley; p 35tl Popperfoto; tr Scope, b UPI/Bettmann; p 39 Ronald Grant; p 41 Popperfoto; p 45 Jonathan Cape Limited; p 47t BBC Photograph library, main Popperfoto; p 49 Ben Ross/Camera Press; p 53t Apple, b Tom Hanley; p 55 Ronald Grant; p 59t Tom Hanley, main Pictorial Press; p 61 Hulton-Deutsch Collection; p 63 main BBC, b Format; p 65t Camera Press, b Hulton; p 69 EMI Records; p 73t Pictorial Press, b K&K/Astrid Kirchherr; p 77 Joseph Tandl/Camera Press; p 79 Richard Carraro; p 81t Hulton, b Rex; p 83 David Redfern; p 85t Hulton, b Rex; p 89t Rex, b Pictorial Press; p 91 Pictorial Press; p 94 Popperfoto; p 96 Camera Press; p 100 main Pictorial Press, b Tom Hanley; p 103t Scope, b Rex; p 105 Popperfoto; p 107t Popperfoto, b Hulton; p 109 Scope; p 111 Popperfoto; p 114 Scope.

Introduction

While making the BBC Radio One series and writing this book, these words of the *Let It Be* film director have often come to mind. Our examination of how Lennon's life and music closely reflected each other is, after all, reliant on John's thoughts, memories and opinions in archive interviews and on the recollections of those near to him.

We have taken ten themes for consideration and interpretation; those which, in our opinion, were quintessential in John Lennon's life. His childhood and contrasting behaviour as a father toward his two sons; his constant, inspiring passion for rock and roll music; the effects of Beatlemania; the surrealism and wit inherent in his books and songs; his adventures in the recording studio; his partnership with Paul McCartney; the influence of his other collaborators – from Stuart Sutcliffe to Allen Klein; his political statements and peace events; his relationships with women, particularly Yoko Ono; and his restless search for contentment through artificial, spiritual and psychological means.

As a merciless mocker of 'intellectual' pretension he would have dismissed this, but we believe that John Lennon was

> *'This is all my opinion: that's all almost any bit of life is, just your opinion.'*
>
> MICHAEL LINDSAY-HOGG

truly a *great artist* of his time. Following in the primordial tradition of mankind's myth-makers, great artists are members of the élite and communicate their insights to the masses. Their startling achievements give them licence to behave eccentrically and their unconventionality is forgiven. John's hectic forty years of highs and lows, elation, sadness, gentleness, cruelty, peace and violence, follow that pattern.

Lennon's music and life were, and will continue to be, an inspiration to generations. Eloquently expressing his ideas and barest emotions in a manner which reached out to millions, the honesty of his work, his humour and his zest are just some of the reasons for his lasting influence. The brilliance of his best records shines on, and our single hope is that this book excites you to listen again, or, indeed, listen for the first time to his music. That experience is a pleasure never to be forgotten.

Kevin Howlett and Mark Lewisohn, August 1990.

Remember

John Winston Lennon was born in Liverpool at 6.30pm on Wednesday 9 October 1940, his middle name reflecting the patriotism rampant in the war-torn city. He was the only child of Julia and Freddy Lennon, a young and fancy-free couple who had tied the knot against the better wishes of their families and who cheerfully described themselves as cinema usherette and seaman on their December 1938 wedding certificate.

When, inevitably, ocean duties beckoned, Freddy slipped easily away from John's life before the child could form even a mental picture of his father – though he was to reappear at two vital stages later on. As for the capricious Julia, the burden of motherhood bore too heavily on her shoulders. Though she later gave birth to three daughters, two of whom she happily brought up, she handed John over to her sister Mary, his indomitable Aunt Mimi, who became his legal guardian.

'He was first brought to me at the house by Julia at ten days old and after that it was his second home until I got him altogether,' Mimi recalls. 'But it was no upheaval for him, coming to me, because you couldn't keep him away from the house. A happy little fellow from morning to night. He was in bed at half-past-six to seven and in the winter I used to leave a light on, on the stairs, to shine into his room.' The already perceptive infant would give his aunt an instant retort, mocking the words of the local ARP warden who enforced total blackout to foil raiding bombers, 'He used to say, "Put that light out, Mimi!", and he'd sing himself to sleep'.

> *'To tell you the truth, when he was born I nearly went off me nut! A boy! Because we were all girls!'*
>
> MARY SMITH,
> JOHN'S AUNT MIMI

Though John's 1970 song 'Working Class Hero' later gave credence to the popular myth that he grew up in humble surroundings, this was far from the truth. From the age of a few months, until he eagerly slid down the social scale into a squalid flat with fellow art college students some 17 years later, John Lennon lived at 251 Menlove Avenue, a spacious semi-detached house set on a busy but leafy thoroughfare in Woolton, one of Liverpool's most pleasant suburbs. Fatherly stability was offered by Mimi's husband, John's Uncle George, who had a respectable job as a local dairyman and proved a kindly ally to the young Lennon until his death in June 1955, aged 52. Though Mimi provided John with a stable, loving environment, she was a stern disciplinarian, determined to equip John with the solid and respectable virtues

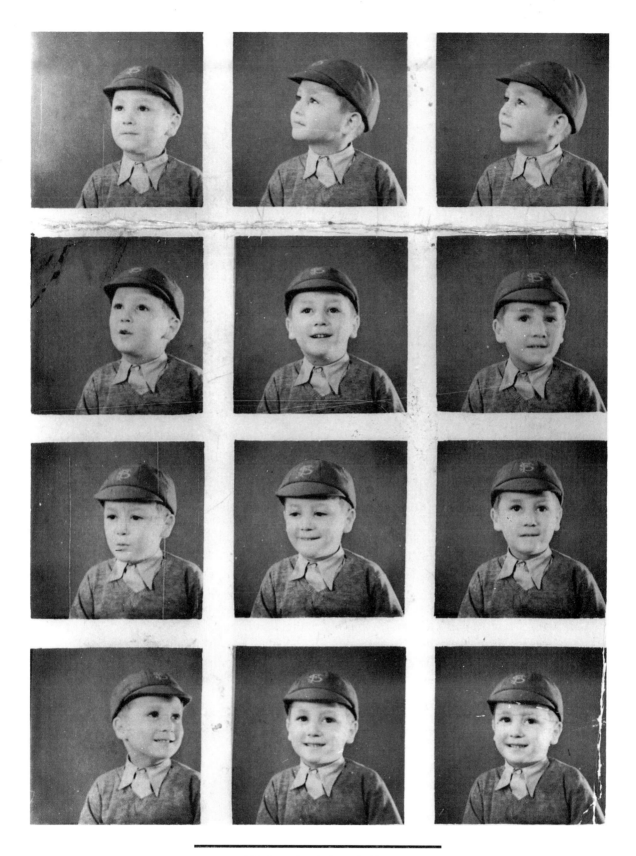

Polyfoto strips of a happy looking
seven-year-old, in the uniform of
Dovedale Primary School

of tidiness, manners and academic achievement.

Mimi faced frequent battles when the increasingly rebellious John reached his teens. 'Mimi was a disciplinarian but a very loving one,' recalls John's step-sister Julia Baird. 'You knew exactly where you stood with her. And he and Mimi did have some humdinger of rows, but Mimi was rowing on his behalf. She was doing what any mother would do. But John had a cop-out and it happened to be his own mother . . . [she] did encourage him really. My mother was fey, eccentric, the artist.'

Her high spirits and devil-may-care attitude were in sharp contrast to her older sister Mimi's outlook. During his teens, John was a frequent visitor at his mother's house, where he adored her fun-loving pranks. His 1968 song 'Julia' evokes the admiration he also had for her physical beauty, 'Her hair of floating sky is shimmering, glimmering in the sun', an allusion to her eye-catching auburn hair.

Julia's life ended abruptly in July 1958 when she was knocked down by a car a few yards from Mimi's house. John, ironically, was visiting his step-sisters at the time. Nonetheless, the proximity of her fatal accident to his home – he could see the spot from an upper-storey window – must have caused him added and persistent anguish. He was just 17-years-old when she died.

With such a tumultuous upbringing – he had seen his mother, initially, just as a relative, but had later come to idolise her as a parent – it is easy to see why her death was so emotionally destroying for him.

'He was devastated,' remembers Paul McCartney, whose own mother had died of cancer in 1956, when he was 14, 'He loved his mum more than anything. She was a very beautiful woman and when you're the son of a very beautiful woman it's got to add something. But at that age you're not allowed to be devastated, particularly not teenage boys. You just shrug it off. I know we had private tears. It's not that either of us were remotely hard-hearted about it – it shattered us – but we knew you had to get on with your life. I'm sure I formed shells and barriers during that period which I've got to this day. We were both wounded animals, and just looking at each other we knew the pain we were feeling. But we weren't going to break down and cry because you just didn't do that kind of thing.'

It took another twelve years for John Lennon to realise and release this pent-up pain with a unique form of psychiatry called Primal Therapy which unlocked the door to his childhood emotions. It was in the spring of 1970 that John and Yoko Ono went to Los Angeles to undertake a course at the Primal Institute, founded and run by Doctors Arthur and Vivian Janov. 'The therapy is about releasing the tension and the repressed pain of early childhood,' explains Vivian Janov. 'That release comes through talking about your life, crying about the pain . . . and people come to feeling very cleansed, very free and very knowledgeable about what really happened to them when they were children. People actually re-live the painful scenes of their life and express the feelings they didn't really express when they were children, and that's what's so therapeutic.'

Primal Therapy had a penetrating effect on John Lennon, and when his stripped-bare emotions found expression on his first post-Beatles album, the record-buying public was similarly shaken. The first track, 'Mother', held nothing back:

Mother, you had me, But I never had you.
I wanted you, You didn't want me.
Father, you left me, But I never left you.
I needed you, You didn't need me.

October 1950, aged ten, in smart blazer, shorts and pulled-up striped socks outside 'Mendips', his Aunt Mimi and Uncle George's house at 251 Menlove Avenue, Woolton, Liverpool, where he was brought up

John's indomitable Aunt Mimi, in full flow before a stunning portrait taken of Lennon by Astrid Kirchherr, fiancée of Stuart Sutcliffe, John's closest friend and former Beatles' bassist

11

And the song ended with a pleading line, screamed over and over by Lennon with an all too real, heart-rending intensity:

Mama don't go! Daddy come home!

The album's closing track was perhaps even more chilling and, in its brevity, so utterly final. Titled 'My Mummy's Dead', he sang:

I can't explain so much pain,
I could never show it,
My mummy's dead.

'If you listen to the Primal album, *John Lennon/Plastic Ono Band*,' says Vivian Janov, 'that is a very deep, central pain for him; his loss and separation. People think that Primal is that you fall down on the floor screaming for your mummy every ten minutes. That's not really true. You can have that core pain stimulated as an adult by another loved person leaving you. I think that he really needed to be near someone close and John's Primal statement, one of several basic ones, was "Mother you had me, I never had you", the most important and basic for all babies. We got the record here and it was explosive, we played it one evening at the Primal Institute and people just fell over, it was so moving. The power of the words and the music to our patients was just the most tremendous thing. It was awesome.'

Primal Therapy provided John with more than just the opportunity to exorcise the mental anguish of his childhood, or the means to make a magnificent rock album. It also afforded a release from the recent emotional turmoil that had beset his life. Between 1968 and 1970 John had divorced first wife Cynthia, married Yoko, lost regular contact with his first son Julian, and seen the Beatles split amid much rancour over business and personal affairs.

As an inseparable couple, John and Yoko had been openly vilified and criticised by a hostile, even racist, press and public, were drained from heroin addiction and their withdrawal from it, and after two years of the closest of relationships were tiring even of each other's 24-hours-a-day companionship. For John, the discovery that his emotional trauma was deeply rooted in his childhood experience was both enlightening and healing. 'I think that Primal Therapy did a lot of good for us,' declares Yoko, because 'John was able to cry it was a very good thing for him.'

Some painful aspects of his childhood remained in place. One was that John could not tolerate being left alone after an argument. 'He said that was the one thing he hated the most,' continues Yoko. 'He would say, "Mimi don't leave me!" because when they argued Mimi would just go out of the room. So when he was being argumentative or something, if I had left the room that would have destroyed him. At least, when he did Primal Therapy, he realised that his anger was coming from something that he felt a long time ago. I was only an excuse to bring it out. Most people do have their violent side, [but] he would never punch me, he would just bring the pillow and punch the pillow in front of me and then he'd be screaming, and after the screaming was over he'd say "OK, that was that. Well, anyone for tea?"'

The fact that John would often refer to Yoko as 'Mother' has led to speculation that she may have replaced Mimi as a maternal figure. The Lennons' close friend, broadcaster Elliot Mintz, observes, 'I'd be willing to read more into it than less. He would never *dream* of referring to Yoko as his "old lady" or his "gal" or his "chick" or any of that stuff. "Mother" seemed much more all encompassing. And I also saw the way he held her, touched her, moved with her. I think we would not be far off the mark by reading a little bit more into the revelation of "Mother".'

Though John may have found a surrogate 'Mother', his other parent was still very much alive. Father and son had last been in contact in the summer of 1946 when Freddy had reappeared in Liverpool, intent on taking his son away with him, perhaps even to New Zealand. They were allowed to go on a day trip to Blackpool together and Freddy extended this to several days without permission, whereupon a concerned Julia tracked them down. There, on the promenade, the parents handed five-year-old John a tug-of-love ultimatum guaranteed to torment a child: he could stay with his father, live abroad and never see his mother, Aunt Mimi or Uncle George again, or he could return with Julia to Liverpool. John's first choice, since he had had such fun in Blackpool, was to stay with Freddy. However, when Julia began to walk out of John's life, he ran after her sobbing the words 'Mummy don't go! Mummy don't go!' which would haunt him anew twenty-five years later. He wouldn't hear of his father again until 1964, when Freddy suddenly popped up in the newspapers as the poor, abandoned parent of a rich and famous pop star.

'My father left me when I was a kid,' John recalled in an interview with Elliot Mintz in January 1976. 'I didn't see him until I made it and he sort of blackmailed his way into my life through the press. I refused to see him and then I finally let him in, started supporting him, looking after him. Then I went to [Primal] Therapy and remembered how furious I was in the depth of my soul, about being left as a child. I mean, I understand people leaving their children because they can't cope, but you don't understand when you're feeling your own misery. So I came

out of therapy and told him to get the hell out, and he did, and I wish I hadn't, really, because, you know, everybody has their problems, including wayward fathers. I'm a bit older now and I understand the pressure of having children and why people can't cope with their responsibility. I regret it, and if he ever turns up I will be reasonable again.'

Ironically, John and Freddy were reconciled by telephone just three months after the interview, when Freddy was on his death-bed. He died on 1 April 1976 in Brighton, having just managed to re-establish contact with his son in distant New York.

John himself had become a father on 8 April 1963 when first wife Cynthia gave birth to a son, John Charles Julian Lennon, to be known as Julian. But despite any good paternal intentions he may have felt, John simply could not play much part in Julian's baby years while living the ultra-frenetic and hectic life of a Beatle. 'I was touring the world,' recalled John in later years, 'I would come home and there'd be a boy there with whom I had no relationship whatsoever. It was a strange child in the house. I'd come back from Australia and he'd be a different size. I wouldn't even recognise the way he looked half the time.'

'I took it for granted that that's how things were,' recalls Julian. 'There was always a thousand people around the house so I was always occupied with someone or another. So if dad disappeared, I didn't really notice. I vaguely remember . . . he used to take me for bike rides down to see Ringo [who lived on the same Weybridge estate], there was a time when I remember standing on the roof of the house with dad, with those little balsa-wood planes with rubber bands, sending them off into the sunset. There are times I remember swimming, walking around the fields . . .'

Even when Beatlemania was dissipating, John found himself distanced from Julian. His 1968 divorce from Cynthia granted custody of their only child to the mother, and father and son went through a period when contact was very sporadic. It was the intervention of Dr Arthur Janov that brought about a reunion. 'Arthur recommended that an important experience for John would be to visit Julian, because he had not been particularly physically close to his son,' states Vivian Janov. 'That was a very strong, emotional day for him because when you start unravelling your own pain you begin to really be able to see your children's pain.'

Thanks to Janov, a father and son link was forged anew, and John and Julian's get-togethers assumed greater frequency. 'When mum and dad separated and he was living in Tittenhurst Park [John and Yoko's house, near Ascot] I used to go and see him at the weekends,' remembers Julian. 'There were 99 acres of fields to be an idiot with him, and a man-made lake, a golf-cart, a studio. For some reason, though, they put me in this spare bedroom that was way down the hallway. I never understood why he put me there . . . there was a room closer. There was one night when I was particularly scared because I thought I heard or felt something and I ran up and started banging on their door and it was locked. And he woke up and just said "Go back to sleep."'

In September 1971, John and Julian's relationship suffered its biggest blow of all, when John and Yoko went to live in the USA, never to return to England. Though they kept a modicum of contact through letters and tapes, new bridges had to be built when Julian, now almost eleven, first journeyed to Los Angeles to stay with his father in 1974. The architect this time was not Arthur Janov, however, but John's girlfriend May Pang.

'It was the first time he had seen Julian in three years,' recalls Pang. 'I remember Yoko saying to me that he would have to see Julian at one point, and I guessed that I pushed that a lot because I believe that, whether they're separated, divorced or together, you have to have the love from both parents.' 'I think he was a little uncomfortable with me, didn't know how to deal with me,' says Julian of that first US visit. 'He wasn't relaxed or settled by any means. I used to laugh a lot in those days, this really annoying laugh, and I remember being shouted at quite a number of times for laughing too much. That was scary, in fact I got a bit worried. When dad shouted at you you knew you were being shouted at. But he calmed down after that.'

It was during one such visit to see his father in America, a decidedly more happy occasion, that Julian made his recording debut. John had already encouraged his son's interest in music by sending him guitars and a drum machine across the Atlantic. In July 1974, while he was making *Walls And Bridges* John invited Julian to join in on a brief cover version of Lee Dorsey's 1961 hit 'Ya Ya'. 'The engineers just pressed the "record" button and that was that,' recalls Julian, who was very surprised to receive a finished album with this impromptu number tacked on the end. 'I went "Cor, that's me and dad!" It meant a lot.'

After a 16-month separation, John and Yoko were reunited at the beginning of 1975, anxious to have a child of their own. Yoko had conceived three times between 1968 and 1970 but miscarried on each occasion due to their remarkably hectic lifestyle and, some would allege, their use of too many artificial stimulants. Speaking to the BBC's Andy Peebles in 1980, John

A 1967 study of four-year-old Julian
with his father in Kenwood, the Lennons'
house in Weybridge, Surrey

'There were 99 acres of fields in which to be an idiot with
him . . .' Eight-year-old Julian holds on during a rare visit
to see his father at Tittenhurst Park, Ascot, 1971

recalled the misery of these miscarriages. 'It turned out that an English doctor told me [there was] something wrong with my sperm, because of the hard life I'd led, and he said that we could never have a baby because of me. But we met a Chinese acupuncturist in San Francisco who said, "I tell you how you have baby: you just be good boy, eat well, no drugs, no drink ..." and that's what I did and we had a baby.'

Sean Taro Ono Lennon was born in New York City on his proud father's 35th birthday, 9 October 1975, and John was determined to make up for his previous shortcomings as a parent. For though it cannot be said that he had ever abandoned Julian as Freddy had once deserted him, John had certainly played all too small a role in Julian's life. Suddenly free of contractual obligations, John gave up the music business and retired from public life, devoting his next five years to ensuring that Sean had the best start that a father could give.

Elliot Mintz, who had witnessed some wild and immature behaviour during John's separation from Yoko, visited the new parents in New York when Sean was ten weeks old, and was struck by the great contrast between the old and new John. 'It was night and day,' he smiles. 'He was alive, centred and of course, the attention given to that little boy was amazing. John walked me over to this little area where Sean was and was very concerned about people breathing germs on him. Perhaps [this was] the concern that was just not there with Julian ...'

'I do recall a lot of attention being paid to Sean,' says Julian, 'and obviously I felt a little jealous. And still do, in some way, feeling that I missed out. I always went to see him, he never came to see me. But just before "what happened" [John's death] happened I had said, "Well, I think it's

about time I should come over, I'm finished with school now ..."'

When John and Yoko returned to active recording in the late summer of 1980, they were determined not to break the strong core of family life to which Sean had grown so accustomed. Though Julian had never been taken to a single Beatles' recording session at Abbey Road, Sean would regularly visit his parents at work at the Hit Factory studios on Manhattan. 'He was a terrific dad,' recalls *Double Fantasy* co-producer Jack Douglas. 'Sean would sit on his lap and he would let him play with the faders and equalisers and limiters.'

Sean was five years and two months old when John was murdered, so his memories of his father are understandably vague. 'I remember just typical father/son things, like playing, talking about whatever I wanted to talk about. Learning how to eat, singing, playing in general. What else do you do when you're a child but play with your father? And that's what I did and that's what I remember. Good times.' (It is a remarkable coincidence that John was abandoned by his father, Julian lost regular contact with *his* father, and Sean's father was cruelly snatched from him, all at five years' old.)

Pleased that Julian had an affinity for music, John considered it vital to instil his second son with a strong sense of rhythm, especially after he had observed how black nurses at the hospital would dance babies around the room while feeding them, listening to R&B or disco radio stations. 'So whenever I fed him I put on the rock and roll or the R&B and danced with him. Now he can dance like nothing on earth,' John proudly reported in December 1980. 'He has perfect pitch, he's into "Hound Dog", and he knows "Be-Bop-A-Lula" backwards.'

Adults the world over testify that being parents can give them a fuller

The self-proclaimed 'house-husband period'. The man who
once entertained millions with his guitar is now a model
father, delighting an audience of two

understanding of their own childhood and rekindle long-forgotten memories of it. This was especially true for John. '[He remembered] little games he used to play when he was a child, like "There's the church, there's the steeple, open the doors, there's the people", or singing "Liverpool Lou" to Sean when he went to sleep,' recalls Yoko.

'Through Sean he was starting to remember his own childhood and he would tell stories about it, not the horrible ones but "Oh, that's the song I was taught . . ." We would go to the docks and the cab driver would be speaking with a very heavy Brooklyn or Bronx accent and John would say, "The Brooklyn accent is like the Liverpool accent! Did I come back, after all this trip, to Liverpool?" So you've got to understand, John was coming all the way back to his childhood, and he was very happy about that.'

Rock And Roll Music

'*I like rock and roll, man,
I don't like much else. That's
what inspired me to
play music. There's nothing
conceptually better than
rock and roll. No group, be
it Beatles, Dylan or Stones,
has ever improved on
"Whole Lotta Shakin'"*,
for my money.'

JOHN LENNON

ock and roll was not the first type of music to assault the ears of John Lennon, but it was certainly the first to capture his heart and soul. It was raw, energetic, sexy, mysterious and rebellious, vital new qualities for a fiercely individual and unconventional teenager. It moved him to pick up a guitar and remained the bedrock of his adult life.

Though he would later examine the roots of this new type of music – and uncover its genesis in American blues and country and western – the 15-year-old Lennon cared only for the spine-tingling *sound* when he first heard Elvis Presley's 'Heartbreak Hotel' in 1956. It was like no other he had ever heard, igniting his senses and firing his creative spirit.

Aunt Mimi had no time for such musical vulgarity, but John was encouraged by his young-at-heart mother, Julia, living nearby with the father of John's two stepsisters. 'My mother played all sorts of instruments,' recalls the elder, also named Julia, now Julia Baird. 'She played the banjo – which she was teaching to John – the piano, the harmonica, the piano accordion, and she sang all the time.' John undoubtedly learned much from his mother. When first playing the guitar, he had to be weaned off banjo chords by Paul McCartney, and though it was Bruce Channel's harmonica player Delbert McClinton who inspired John to use that instrument on all of the early Beatles' records, it is also likely that he acquired an interest in it from his mother.

Most importantly, Julia had a taste for rock and roll. 'I just remember my dad coming in and saying, "Well, I've got it. Is this what you wanted?",' recalls Julia Baird. 'She put it on and it was "Heartbreak Hotel" and she said "Yes, yes, that's it, that's it!". She loved Elvis.'

Although John's passion for rock and roll was ferocious, it was not this alone that prompted him to form a group and play in public. The other catalyst was skiffle, a cheap and cheerful British imitation of US folk music played with a chugging rhythm. Skiffle's prime exponent was Lonnie Donegan and its chief anthem, 'Rock Island Line', was an old American blues number. Because of its simple instrumental requirements, skiffle could be played by anyone, even the impoverished. Thousands of combos quickly formed all over Britain, Liverpool being a particular hotbed of activity. John Lennon and some cronies from the Quarry Bank High School formed the Quarry Men, soon to be supplemented by Paul McCartney and George Harrison from another school.

Still, rock and roll remained at the root of John's and the others' passion for music and for every skiffling 'Cumberland Gap' or 'Maggie May' he would slip in 'Be-Bop-A-Lula' or 'Hound Dog'. On one occasion, when the Quarry Men played at the Cavern Club, then a jazz preserve but tolerating skiffle because of its quasi-jazz origins, a curt note from the management, 'Cut out the bloody rock', was handed up to Lennon while onstage. When the skiffle fad perished in 1958 the Quarry Men never looked back and merely stepped up the gas on the rock and roll music.

Elvis Presley was not the only hero. There was also Gene Vincent, Little Richard, Jerry Lee Lewis, Chuck Berry, Eddie Cochran, Carl Perkins, Lloyd Price, Larry Williams and Buddy Holly, whose wearing of black horn-rimmed spectacles persuaded Lennon, the embarrassed teenager several thousand miles away across the Atlantic, to remove his glasses from his pocket and wear them, albeit temporarily.

But rock and roll meant more than music; it was a way of life, in which the correct dress was vital. In Britain, rockers with a rebellious streak modelled their clothing after gentlemen's attire in the Edwardian era, with long jackets and ultra-tight 'drainpipe' trousers, hence they became Teddy Boys, whose tough street image did occasionally translate into violence. John was every inch a 'Ted', yet in his chameleonic way could also switch to the other extreme. 'I was always torn between being a Teddy Boy and an art student,' John told the BBC in 1973. 'One week I'd go to art school with my art school scarf on and my hair down and the next week I'd go with the leather jacket and tight jeans. So I could never make up my mind ... I've always been a little bit arty.'

'The first time he came to the college [Liverpool College of Art] in September 1957, I noted him straight away because he stood out in the crowd,' recalls fellow-student Bill Harry, later to launch the important and early pop paper *Mersey Beat*. 'He had his DA haircut [a style that looked not unlike a duck's arse, hence the moniker] and looked like a Teddy Boy. Everyone else was wearing duffel coats and polo-neck sweaters, and I thought, "All these people are supposed to be so unconventional and they're all conventionally dressed, and there's John, he looks completely different".'

The art college was a good place for the Quarry Men to rehearse, being next door to the Liverpool Institute, where Paul McCartney and George Harrison studied. Lunchtimes would see Paul and George nip across to the life-rooms with their guitars for a quick recuperative blast of Chuck Berry. Other rehearsals took place wherever space permitted. 'They'd use Mimi's porch because of how it echoed,' recalls Julia Baird, 'or our bathroom, standing with their feet up on the side of the bath, because of the acoustics in there.'

Rock and roll was in the bloodstream of these boys. They *lived* for it, and in Britain its attraction was all the greater for being rather like forbidden fruit. There was no commercial radio, very little rock on the BBC, practically none on television, no videos, almost no pop/rock reporting in the daily newspapers, no glossy magazines, no logo-emblazoned T-shirts, no discotheques and very few rock shows visiting town. Like the other members of the Quarry Men and teenagers all over Britain, John would hear his rock under the bedcovers, his ear pressed tight to the wireless, straining to catch the fading late-night sounds beamed across Northern Europe from Radio Luxembourg.

Of course, another way to hear the

Above Saturday 22 June 1957, playing from the back of a coal lorry, sixteen-year-old John Lennon leads his Quarry Men through a skiffle number during an open-air party in Rosebery Street, Liverpool. Two weeks later he met Paul McCartney for the first time

Left John Lennon, the arch-rocker, photographed at a fancy-dress party in London in December 1967 but reminiscent of Liverpool ten years earlier

Far left Elvis Presley, inspirational for the young rocker John

music was to buy it. However, John, Paul and George were still students, and there was never much cash around. Paul McCartney has recalled how he might hear of someone the other side of town owning a certain record – The Coasters' 'Searchin' ', for one – and how he would travel all the way over to this stranger's house, invite himself in, and sit listening to the song, over and over, noting down the words and trying to discern the chords.

As the group's repertoire grew, so each member devoted himself to the work of his American idols. John usually made sure that he bagged Chuck Berry and Gene Vincent's material, Paul specialised in Little Richard and Elvis Presley while George opted to concentrate on rockabilly heroes like Carl Perkins.

The Quarry Men metamorphosed into the Beatles during 1960, on the eve of their first, longest and most formative trip to Hamburg in Germany. They played there for four and a half hours a night on week-days and six hours a night at weekends for more than 100 consecutive nights, between August and November. They had left Liverpool as just another group, of a significantly lower standard than the city's best. In Hamburg, however, while belting out rock and roll music to the hard-drinking patrons of seedy Reeperbahn night-clubs, the Beatles moulded their talents and crafted their distinctive sound which would eventually rock the world. 'We were a good live band then,' John Lennon told friend and DJ Elliot Mintz in January 1976, 'I enjoyed that. We worked and played long hours, which was good at that age, when you can get work.'

Staying awake during such long stints meant surviving on a diet of cheap food, sex, pills and plenty of alcohol, the classic rock and roll lifestyle. Dressed in their tight jeans, leather jackets and pointed-toe cowboy boots, the Beatles emitted a fierce, uncompromising look, comple-mented by their wild, unpredictable behaviour. John not only sang 'Be-Bop-A-Lula', he emulated the menacing behav-iour of Gene Vincent. Occasionally, things could get out of hand. Horst Fascher, who worked in the clubs, remembers John buying a pig at a market, putting a dog-collar around its neck and pulling it around the streets. On another occasion he donned a monkey suit, played onstage and then left the club, terrorising folk in the street. 'They went to another club and he scared people to death, jumping on the tables and screaming like a monkey, and people were running out of the clubs,' recalls Fascher.

This type of behaviour was bound to attract the attention of the police, even in Hamburg, a city noted for excess. When George Harrison, at 17, was found to be under age for working in a night-club, and when Paul McCartney and drummer Pete Best started a small fire inside their former lodgings, the police stepped in and all three were deported. 'There were times when I despaired,' John Lennon told Elliot Mintz 16 years later. 'I was left there on my own and came home with no money and carrying amplifiers and guitars, and I thought "Is this what I want to do ... night-clubs, seedy scenes, being deported? Should I continue doing this?" ' But after a few days in which even the other Beatles were not told of his return to Liverpool, John did call and reunite the group for some concerts over Christmas 1960. It was these shows, one in particular in north Liverpool, at the Litherland Town Hall on 27 December, that revealed just how vastly the group had improved in Hamburg.

In January 1961 the Beatles began an unrelenting schedule of live engagements, sometimes performing at three different venues on the same day, one at lunchtime and two in the evening. Their most loyal following was built at the Cavern Club, the subterranean dive where Quarry Man John had once been admonished for playing rock and roll. Now the club was almost exclusively devoted to rock music, and the Beatles became its premier act, playing almost 300 shows there: lunchtimes, evenings and marathon all-night sessions, between February 1961 and August 1963. 'We were performers in Liverpool, Hamburg and round the dance halls,' John Lennon told Jann Wenner of *Rolling Stone* in 1970, 'and what we generated was fantastic, and when we played straight rock there was no one to touch us in Britain. But as soon as we made it the rough edges were knocked off.'

The Beatles' tough-looking image and their uncompromising attitude onstage – drinking, eating, swearing, doing Nazi goose-steps – all disappeared when Brian Epstein became their manager. He knew that, in Britain in the early 1960s, one had to conform, at least relatively so, to the accepted show business norm: one certainly had to dress smart, present songs in an orderly fashion and, if possible, bow at the end of numbers. The Beatles knew it too, and despite John Lennon's protestations about 'selling out when we made it', voiced with some regularity from the safe distance of the 1970s, he himself, along with the other Beatles, had made a definite, conscious decision to try this approach. Though it cannot be claimed that they had a master plan, it was easier, surely, to subvert from within, and to change such archaic pop practices once they were in a strong position, than to be rejected in the first place for being so unconventional.

Lennon knew that being managed by Brian Epstein meant suppressing some of his wilder tendencies in public. 'John came running up to see me at the office,'

remembers Bill Harry, speaking of the *Mersey Beat* newspaper he edited. 'He said, "All those pictures I gave you of me in Hamburg, I've got to have them back". These were photographs of John standing in his underpants on the corner of the Reeperbahn reading a newspaper, or onstage with a toilet-seat around his neck. John was furious when the Rolling Stones came around with their rough, raw image and seemed to get away with it. He said "That's what *we* were like."'

In truth, this Rolling Stones' image was as carefully crafted by mentor Andrew Oldham as Brian Epstein tailored the Beatles' public attitude and appearance. It was consciously manufactured by Oldham, who had briefly worked for Epstein, to be the very antithesis of the Beatles. Though Lennon might have craved to be as publicly raunchy as the Rolling Stones, it is quite conceivable that the Stones, despite their obvious talent, may have remained undiscovered were it not for the Beatles – in their smart suits – creating such a musical boom in Britain in the early 1960s.

This boom began in February 1963, when the Beatles first hit number one on the British singles chart with 'Please Please Me'*. Because of this success, the group returned to the studio on 11 February 1963 to record an album, also titled *Please Please Me*. It showed that, if their live appearances *had* been sanitised, the Beatles had not completely rejected their rock and roll roots. The album grasped the sound of the group before national and then international fame overtook them. Speaking in 1976 John recalled, 'It was the nearest thing to trying to capture us live, the nearest thing to how we sounded in Hamburg or Liverpool, the nearest to what we sounded like before we became the clever Beatles.'

The last song on *Please Please Me* was

---

* There were five UK national charts published then: it hit the top in four of them, but not the fifth, which – though no more valid or important than the others – happens to be the one used by Guinness for its widely quoted *British Hit Singles* book.

'Twist And Shout', a cover of the Isley Brothers' US hit from July 1962. A live, first-take recording, Lennon's blistering vocal performance has gone down as one of the greatest moments in rock history. Lennon himself, typically, remembered it differently. 'It nearly killed me, it was the last song after 12 hours of singing and being in a recording studio. I was always bitterly ashamed of it because I could sing it better than that.'

When it came to actual live performances, fame for a pop act in those days, whether in Britain or America, meant joining 'package tours', where a string of as many as six or seven acts would travel together by coach to theatres (often cinemas in Britain) and play two separate concerts per evening, each act singing perhaps only three or four songs. Even the top-of-the-bill act might play for only 20 or 25 minutes. For the Beatles, this meant an end to hours of exhilarating rock and roll and the beginning of short, play-the-hits shows and – from mid-1963 – to audiences who could barely hear their efforts through a barrage of shrill screaming.

'By the time the Beatles hit America they could no longer play live or work very well at all,' remembered Lennon in a US interview some years later. 'In Hamburg and Liverpool we'd been used to playing six or eight hours a day ... nobody played less than two or three hours for any gig. By the time we got here we'd got down to playing 20 minutes. That's why the Beatles were famous for doing 15 minute shows – we could speed it up to 15 minutes. Fifty thousand people would see us and we'd be off in 15 minutes.'

Though the Beatles never ceased being rock musicians, their records after the album *Help!* (the last time they performed anything other than self-composed material) steered away from the rock and roll of their youth. And after 1966, when

they stopped touring, opportunities to play such music disappeared altogether except in studio jamming never meant for release. So in 1969, after the Beatles had ceased working together, John did not hesitate to agree to a sudden invitation to perform in a 'Rock 'n' Roll Revival' concert in Toronto, putting together a makeshift Plastic Ono Band.

'Chuck [Berry] was gonna be there, Jerry Lee was gonna be there, all the great rockers that were still living. We didn't know what to play because we'd never played together before, so on the airplane we were running through these oldies, "Are we doing the Elvis version of 'Blue Suede Shoes' or the Carl Perkins, with the different break at the beginning ...?"' John Lennon, the rocker, was back. 'It wasn't like this set format that I'd been doing with the Beatles, where you go on and do the same numbers – "I Wanna Hold Your Head" – the show lasts 20 minutes, nobody's listening, they're screaming, and the amps are as big as a peanut. I did a couple of songs [in Toronto] that I hadn't done since Liverpool.'

The Toronto gig was followed, three months later, by one at the Lyceum Ballroom in London, in aid of UNICEF. Playing with the Plastic Ono Band was certainly easier than playing with the Beatles. As John told the BBC reporter David Bellan, 'They expect Buddha or Mohammed to come on and play ... that's the fear that the Beatles have. So much is expected of us. Playing isn't the problem, it's going on as the Beatles that's the problem.'

As the 1970s dawned and the Beatles broke-up, John became like any other person smitten by rock and roll: nostalgic for the music of his youth. 'You just get any musician over 26 sitting down with me and it's all about "Remember ...?". That's our era, we're already old folks

Rock and roll wasn't all glamour. When the Beatles played
their first ever engagement in the south of England – at
the Palais Ballroom in Aldershot, Hampshire on
9 December 1961 – only eighteen people showed up

The leather-clad Beatles during another lunchtime session
in the Cavern Club, Liverpool, December 1961; on this
occasion they provided the backing for visiting R&B singer
Davy Jones

saying "Those were the days!"' Though John always professed to being 'a record man', preferring the essential sound of the original disc to a live performance, he was intrigued when, at the start of his 'lost weekend' period in late 1973, his friend Elliot Mintz offered him the opportunity to see Jerry Lee Lewis in concert at the Roxy, a club in Hollywood. 'He was as excited as a child going to the circus,' laughs Mintz. 'Jerry did all his tunes, lifted his foot and put it on the piano keys and it was thrilling.' The show ended and he and John went backstage. 'He was as nervous as somebody about to meet John Lennon. I simply said, "Jerry, I'd like you to meet John Lennon; John, Jerry Lee Lewis", and John fell down on his knees and started kissing Jerry Lee's shoes. And Jerry Lee Lewis put his hand out and touched John's shoulders and said, "Now now son, no need for that, that's just fine son, just fine ..."'

Apple Records' promotions man, Tony King, tells a similar, though more poignant story, about taking John to see Fats Domino in cabaret at a Las Vegas hotel during the same period. 'He was very sad to see Fats Domino in a second-class lounge, with lots of people talking and clinking glasses. He was saying, "God, it's horrible isn't it? That's one of my heroes up there and there's all these idiots drinking. They don't realise who he is." And afterwards John met Fats, and Fats was terribly aware of who John was and was being very sweet to him, and John turned around and said, "Hey, you don't have to be like this to me. It's me who should be paying *you* the attention. *You're* the one!" That really upset him.'

The perfect evocation of John's 'lost weekend' period was his *Rock 'n' Roll* album. Separated from Yoko at the time, John launched into the making of an album of his rock favourites, telling

producer Phil Spector, whose work on early rock tracks Lennon enormously admired, that he wanted to record as had Spector's wife, Ronnie, of the Ronettes – that is, with no production involvement, merely as a performer. 'I'd used Spector before,' John told the BBC's Bob Harris in 1975, 'but I'd always controlled it and been co-producer. I said "Look, I'm Ronnie on this one, I just wanna sing, I don't wanna know nothing about nothing ..."'

But there was little chance of Lennon knowing nothing about nothing. Despite the large quantities of alcohol and other substances consumed at the Los Angeles sessions he could not turn a blind eye to the increasingly undisciplined events at the nightly tapings. 'They collapsed into mania,' John recalled, only half-smiling. 'It definitely got crazy. There were 28 guys playing a night and 15 of them were out of their minds, including me.'

In this particular interview, John was reluctant to reveal exactly what had happened, but a picture can now be formed from others who witnessed *Rock 'n' Roll* in the making. 'Those were the wildest sessions that I or anyone will ever go to,' states Tony King. 'They were legendary in Hollywood – there were guns, there were fights, people were being insulted right, left and centre. I think it was Warren Beatty who had a gun put to his head by Phil Spector, John insulted Joni Mitchell.' May Pang, who accompanied John throughout his 16 months apart from Yoko, recalls how Phil Spector set the tone for the sessions, 'Every night he'd be dressed as a butcher, a doctor, a lawyer, a karate expert ...'

The album's recording eventually stopped when, instead of turning up for a session, Phil Spector retreated to the innermost sanctum of his heavily guarded Hollywood home – with all the tapes. 'He called me and said, "I've got the John

The 'Plastic Ono Supergroup' at the Lyceum Ballroom in London, 15 December 1969. The occupant of the white bag was, of course, Yoko

Dean tapes,"' remembered John in 1980. 'I said, "What are you talking about?" "The house is surrounded by helicopters, they're trying to get them. I'm the only one that knows how to tell whether they've been doctored or edited." Well what he was trying to tell me, in his own sweet way, was that he had *my* tapes, not the John Dean Watergate tapes but my tapes, locked in the cellar behind the barbed wire, the Afghan dogs and the machine guns.' (*Rock 'n' Roll* engineer Jimmy Iovine, now a top producer, tells a neat postscript to this bizarre story: 'Years later I did a single with Darlene Love and I said, "Darlene, do you remember when we worked on those Phil Spector sessions together? Well, Phil said he had the Watergate tapes and that's why everything was going crazy." And she says, "He did, I heard 'em ..."'')

It was not until July 1974 that John retrieved his tapes, considering only four tracks worthy of rescue. To complete the album he returned to the studio – this time in New York and without the enigmatic Phil Spector – and polished off the remaining nine tracks in just five days, a pace

reminiscent of the early Beatles' work. *Rock 'n' Roll* was finally issued in February 1975, a sensational way to end another key era in his life, the 'house-husband' phase being just around the corner. 'I looked at the cover which I'd chosen, which is a picture of me in Hamburg from 1961, and I thought, "Is this some kind of a karmic thing? I'm ending as I started, singing this straight rock and roll stuff."'

When John returned to recording in 1980 with *Double Fantasy* it was obvious that, though his personality had mellowed, his music remained rooted in his youthful rock and roll years, describing the opening single, '(Just Like) Starting Over', as his 'Elvis/Orbison track', while heroes like Buddy Holly continued to exert a clear influence on his guitar and vocal style. Though he was the perennial chameleon, one thing certain about John Lennon is that rock and roll would have always remained the essential ingredient in his music, just as it had ever since Elvis had sung the opening line of 'Heartbreak Hotel' – 'Well since my baby left me ...' – at him from across the Atlantic in 1956.

Help!

Beatlemania! Britain, indeed the world, had never seen anything like it; Beatlemania remains the yardstick against which all other forms of fan-worship are measured. Beatlemania was a twentieth-century phenomenon. But, like all phenomena, it remains almost impossible to analyse or define. Beatlemania was simply . . . Beatlemania.

The word was coined by Fleet Street journalists in the autumn of 1963, when the Beatles appeared in two events that represented what was then the pinnacle of British show business – though, by today's standards, they seem decidedly middle-of-the-road for a rock act – the TV variety show *Val Parnell's Sunday Night At The London Palladium* and the Royal Command Performance, attended by bejewelled royal personages and watched by millions on TV. Journalists were delighted to note the crowds of frantic, wildly screaming teenage girls who rather upstaged these staid adult events, especially when they realised that it was a British act invoking such pandemonium, not Frank Sinatra, not Johnnie Ray, not Bill Haley, not Elvis Presley on film. Though Cliff Richard too could provoke the screams, here was something

> '*Everybody wants the image to carry on. The press . . . want the free drinks and the free whores and the fun. Everybody wants to keep on the bandwagon. We were the Caesars. Who was going to knock us when there's a million pounds to be made?*'
>
> JOHN LENNON

altogether new, bright, fresh and talented.

Having sought fame and success for several years, John, Paul, George and Ringo – very soon to be four instantly recognisable names, wherever the country, whatever the language – were naturally flattered by such an overwhelming response to their music and personalities, and were, initially, quite happy to keep the ball rolling. They consented to all that the public and the Beatles' astute manager Brian Epstein asked of them – an exhausting schedule of radio, TV and concert appearances, contrived photo sessions and personal appearances.

In one scarcely believable two-week visit in February 1964, the Beatles conquered America, not only the world's most important music and show business territory but one previously inpenetrable to foreign acts. With the force of encouraging slaps still tingling on his shoulder, and a proud British press watching his every move, Cliff Richard had ventured to the United States in January 1960 as the UK's hottest pop property – and flopped, appearing way down on a multi-act bill headed by Frankie Avalon. The Beatles' visit was in complete contrast to Cliff's woeful reception; they assaulted the continent in such dynamic fashion that the resulting shock-waves were felt for years afterwards.

Arranged in November 1963, when Brian Epstein negotiated three appearances on the top-rated TV variety programme *The Ed Sullivan Show*, the Beatles were blessed with the remarkable coincidence of a number one hit single, 'I Want To Hold Your Hand', the day they touched down at New York's Kennedy International Airport, only just re-named from Idlewild by a nation still mourning its 35th president, assassinated eleven weeks previously. Frantic scenes at airports had already been witnessed on four occasions in England, the first when the group returned from a short tour of Sweden in October 1963. Still, as their plane approached Kennedy the Beatles could scarcely believe their eyes – the airport seemed populated by a swarm of ants. At ground level the termites in the terminal were revealed to be 10 000 fans, whose screaming seemed even louder than that encountered elsewhere. Before stepping out of the plane, before playing a note of music, before winning over the hardened US media with their Liverpool wit, the Beatles had broken into the most insular and profitable market of them all. Beatlemania had actually preceded them.

Q: Your fans obviously enjoyed it over there, I assume the press enjoyed it. Did you enjoy it?

George: Yes, it was marvellous, everything.

Q: Did you have a chance to get away from anybody at any time on the trip?

Ringo: He got away from me twice. [Laughter]

Q: Did you ever have a chance, John, to just get away on your own, without anybody recognising you?

John: We borrowed a couple of millionaires' houses . . .

Q: You can afford to buy a couple of millionaires' houses, couldn't you?

John: No, not yet. We'd sooner borrow them, it's cheaper.

Q: What about the taste of the fans over there?

John: We never bit any.

[From the Beatles' press conference at London Airport, on their return from the USA, 22 February 1964]

Though ear-piercing mass adulation was evident in every country visited for concerts by the group between 1964 and 1966 – Australia, Canada, Denmark, France, Hong Kong, Ireland, Italy, Japan, the Netherlands, New Zealand, the Philippines, Spain, Sweden, the USA and West Germany – as well as plenty of other countries *not* granted a concert visit, the American brand of Beatlemania was, like so many other aspects of life there, more whole-hearted, unflagging and intense. But the initial pleasures brought to the Beatles by such adoration were swiftly outweighed by the incessant mayhem. They became prisoners of their own fame, trapped by the very success they had courted through their long nights in the Cavern Club and in Hamburg.

A Hard Day's Night, the group's first feature film, was made at the height of Beatlemania and it marked a refreshing departure from the usual frothy pop films, which were of a poor standard everywhere, nowhere more so than in Britain, where they were laughable beyond any comedy content. Speedily made, for fear that Beatlemania might dissipate, *A Hard Day's Night* energetically captured the essence of the Beatles' lifestyle in early 1964,

The Beatles are welcomed home at London Airport on 22
February 1964. The return was an event of such
magnitude that the BBC screened pictures of it in its
afternoon sports programme *Grandstand*

helped by Alun Owen's short-sharp script and director Richard Lester's cleverly managed camera work and fast-cutting scenes.

'Just after we'd agreed to do it,' recalls Lester, 'they were appearing in Paris. We spent a weekend in the George V hotel with them and the film wrote itself. They'd just come back from Stockholm, and I said to John, "Oh, how did you like it?" and he said "What do you mean like it? It was a car and a room, and a room and a car, and a plane and a car." That was the story of the film.'

Made in black-and-white, *A Hard Day's Night* created a fictionalised Beatlemania that was very like the real thing – indeed during the filming they did encounter the real thing. 'Wherever we went to shoot, within thirty seconds of arriving, even if we were hiding under tents pretending to be workmen, whatever, there would be 2000 kids,' recalls Lester. 'We would have a car drive up, the boys would get out, I would shout "Go", they would do what they were supposed to do and there would be a car waiting at the point where the shot finished, which would take them off. But even with that there was no way we could do a second take, because we would be absolutely jammed up against a building, defending our lives.'

For John Lennon – rapidly tiring of the constraints of Beatlemania, and the dishonesty of being an ever-smiling, fun-loving, mop-topped idol – the down side of *A Hard Day's Night* was that scriptwriter Owen's creation of the Beatles' fictional roles soon became accepted as reality by the public. Talented in so many areas and, in real life, exceedingly hard to pigeon-hole, they became trapped into these stereotyped roles which have proved irresistible – to this day. Speaking to Jann Wenner of *Rolling Stone* in December 1970, John bitterly expressed his opinion of *A Hard Day's Night*, stating, 'We were a bit infuriated by the glibness of it – me witty, Ringo dumb and cute – and were always trying to get it more realistic. But they wouldn't have it. It was a good projection of one façade of us, which was on tour, of us in that situation together, in a hotel, having to perform before people, but we thought it was phony ... it wasn't realistic enough.'

It was a hallmark of the Beatlemania years that such negative opinions remained suppressed, indeed it was not until John, and also George Harrison, openly declared their resentment for much of what had happened from the vantage point of the 1970s that people realised all had not been rosy in the Beatles' garden. Beatlemania was such a powerful animal that, at the time, it would permit only the positive aspects to be highlighted. As John recalled in the same interview with Jann Wenner, mid-1960s Beatles' tours were like the film *Satyricon*: madness on the road, with drugs, whores and orgies, yet even journalists who observed the scenes kept silent, electing to enjoy it while it lasted rather than blow the whistle and destroy not only the Beatles' image but also opportunities to join in the fun.

For the Beatles, undertaking concert tours was becoming simply too tiresome. They scarcely needed the money and certainly would rather stay at home than face weeks of manhandling, imprisonment in hot hotel rooms eating cold cooked meals, and playing concerts at which they could barely hear themselves sing or play above the incessant, full-throated screams. Yet when the circus did come to town they continued, at least until 1965, to smile bravely, and to host press conferences galore for unimaginative, sycophantic journalists.

From *A Hard Day's Night*, with Ringo (left) and actors
Wilfrid Brambell (centre) and Norman Rossington (right);
shot at Twickenham Film Studios, spring 1964

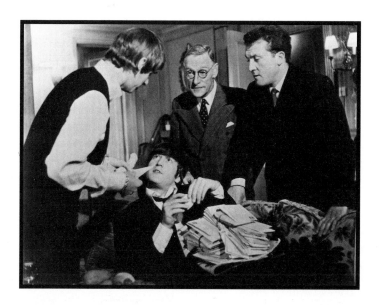

Considering the merits of life on the road – a car, a plane,
a hotel, a dressing-room and a stage – from inside an
Austin Princess, autumn 1964

Q: Do you have any plans for beyond when you are the Beatles?

John: No.

Q: I'd like to ask Mr Lennon why he took up writing and who was his biggest influence in the writing field.

John: I don't know why I took it up, and I haven't got a biggest . . . I suppose Lewis Carroll.
[Laughter]

Paul: That's not funny!

Q: I'd like to know what happened to the colour of John Lennon's hair.

John: Well it's covered in sweat, you see, so it looks darker than it is. It is wet, that's why it looks so different.
[Laughter]

Q: How do you like being a Beatle?

John: It's just great, it's just wonderful, wonderful. It's good. We like it or we'd be the Rolling Stones.

[From the Beatles' Toronto press conference 17 August 1965]

With the benefit of hindsight, it is possible to see clear signs that the group were finding Beatlemania too much to handle. The sleeve of their album *Beatles For Sale*, issued in December 1964, showed not the smiling faces the world knew so well but peering, enquiring, weary young men. The content, too, moved one step beyond happy-go-lucky boy-meets-girl pop material. Lennon's 'Baby's In Black' was almost morbid and his 'I'm A Loser' positively revealing – 'Although I laugh and I act like a clown, beneath this mask I am wearing a frown'.

In the spring of 1965, the group made their second film *Help!*. Shot in colour but lacking the sparkle or invention of *A Hard Day's Night*, it was made during a treadmill period for the group, a time when they could not hope to surpass their glorious successes, only repeat them. Hindsight can tell us, once again, just as it told composer John Lennon, that 'Help!', his catchy title song, was more than just two and a half minutes of great pop music. Asking, literally, for 'help', writing of being 'insecure', 'not so self-assured', 'feeling down' and of independence that had vanished 'in the haze', it was a meaningful plea which was totally overlooked. 'I was in the middle of a trough in *Help!* but you can't see it,' John said in an interview with the BBC in 1975. 'It was less noticeable because you're protected by the image of the power of the Beatles.'

Privately the Beatles were now wiping the smiles off their faces and rejecting numerous offers for concert tours, TV and radio appearances, and especially invitations to perform a second time at the Royal Command Performance. Even when meeting royalty or dignitaries, they were no longer prepared to turn on the charm. When the location shooting for *Help!* moved to the Bahamas, the Beatles were filmed at what appeared to be a remote, derelict army base – but John discovered that the building was actually a hospital, full of handicapped children and old people, inhumanely shut away. That evening, at a dinner held in the Beatles' honour, John raised the matter with the Bahamanian Minister of Finance. Also present was *Help!* actor and the Beatles' friend Victor Spinetti. 'John said, "Is that the way you take care of people? I mean, you're the Minister of Finance, you're doing well, so are you taking care of them?" This fellow said, "Mr Lennon, I am not paid to be the Minister of Finance, my job is an honorary one". And John looked around at all the luxurious trappings of the table, all the soup, the plates of caviar, and said, "Well, you're doing

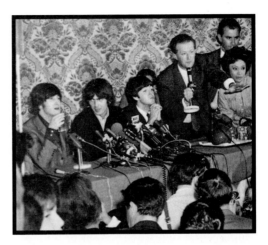

Left The mayhem of a 1965 US Beatles concert, their chauffeur Alf Bicknell spiriting away a fan who broke through the supposedly inpenetrable police cordon

Below Don't mention the war! A typically packed Beatles press conference from their North American tour, 1965

Beatlemania hits the bonfire in the deep South, following John's statement that the Beatles are 'more popular than Jesus'

better than I thought you were doing".'

Speaking to *Rolling Stone* in 1970, Lennon cited this very incident as being typical of the bad side of Beatlemania. 'Those were the most humiliating experiences, like sitting with the Governor of the Bahamas when we were making *Help!*, and being insulted by these jumped-up middle-class bitches and bastards, who would be commenting on our working classness and our manners. And I was always drunk, insulting them. I couldn't take it. It would hurt me. I would go insane and be swearing at them. All that business was awful, it was a fucking humiliation. One has to completely humiliate oneself to be what the Beatles were, and that's what I resent. I mean, I did it, but I didn't know, I didn't foresee, it just happened bit by bit ... till this complete craziness is surrounding you and you're doing exactly what you don't want to do with people you can't stand, the people you hated when you were ten.'

Restless, and noticeably putting on weight, John Lennon was drowning in a sea of excess. Though just 24-years-old, the former Liverpool 'Ted' and art school dropout was now married with a young child and living the fat life out in the comfortable, conservative Weybridge area near London. The traditional trappings of success were never going to satisfy this most individual of men. 'I'm just stopping at it,' said John at this time. 'I'll take my time, I'll get my *real* house when I know what I want.'

In June 1965, in the midst of this phase, later described by John as his 'fat Elvis' period, each of the Beatles was awarded an MBE in the Queen's Birthday Honours List. It was the ultimate seal of establishment approval for four smart-in-appearance yet scruffy-at-heart rock musicians from what had once been unfashionable Liverpool. The group –

especially John – were somewhat embarrassed by the whole episode and certainly didn't feel as grateful as people would have expected. Their flippant and irreverent remarks, which they felt necessary to deflate the whole charade, only fuelled the sense of outrage felt by some previous MBE recipients, a few registering their disgust by returning their precious medals to Buckingham Palace.

The year of 1966 brought a decisive end to this epochal phase in the Beatles' career. The frenzied but peaceful fan worship that typified Beatlemania turned to violence when the group returned to Hamburg to play their first concert in the city for more than three years. There were demonstrations in Tokyo against the Beatles playing at the 'sacred' Budokan venue, and the group were deemed to have 'snubbed' Imelda Marcos, the First Lady of the Philippines, when they failed to attend a presidential palace reception during a concert visit to Manila, a move which, inevitably, produced violent repercussions.

But the biggest storm of them all blew up on the eve of the Beatles' fourth North American concert tour. In an interview with friend and journalist Maureen Cleave, first published in the London *Evening Standard* that March, John reflected that, such was the decline of the church, the Beatles' popularity was now greater than organised religion. 'Christianity will go. It will vanish and shrink. I needn't argue about that; I'm right and I will be proved right. We're more popular than Jesus now. I don't know which will go first – rock 'n' roll or Christianity. Jesus was all right but his disciples were thick and ordinary. It's them twisting it that ruins it for me.'

Though Londoners did not react to the remark, when syndicated to *Datebook*, a US teen magazine, and printed out of context, many Americans did, provoking the fundamentalist Southern states to organise 'Stamp Out The Beatles' campaigns, the burning of records, and the extremist Ku Klux Klan to demonstrate outside Beatles' concerts.

Instead of the usual jovial banalities and meaningless banter, the Beatles faced a far more serious line of questioning during their pre-tour press conference in Chicago in August 1966. Eager to placate yet also to stand his ground and not actually say sorry, John was matter-of-fact when the inevitable questions were put to him. 'I'm not saying that we're *better* or *greater*, or comparing us with Jesus Christ as a person, or God as a thing, or whatever it is. I just said what I said and it was wrong, or was taken wrong. And now it's all this. If I'd said television is more popular than Jesus I might have got away with it.' Later on during the tour, when the rumpus had finally died down, the real Lennon spoke out, referring to the anti-Beatles protesters as 'middle-aged DJs and 12-year-olds burning a pile of LP covers'.

That fourth US concert tour, ending in San Francisco on 29 August 1966, was the Beatles' last. Quite apart from the offstage incidents, the group's onstage musicianship that summer reached its nadir at the very time when, in the recording studio, they were becoming so inventive and caring. Here was the top rock group in the world playing and singing out-of-tune and out-of-time, knowing that – even if the audience could hear – they wouldn't care. The concerts were *events*, the Beatles were there to be gawped and screamed at, not to be listened to. The reception would have been the same no matter how well or badly they performed. Remarkably, the Beatles toured North America simultaneous to the release of *Revolver* without performing a single track from this most innovative of albums and

without even one pre-tour rehearsal session.

'I didn't know what to do,' John told the BBC's Andy Peebles in December 1980. 'What do you do when you don't tour? What the hell do you do all day? That's when I really started considering: what can one do, considering life without the Beatles?'

What the Beatles did was to direct their energies into the recording studio. It had always been a refuge for them, a private place in a very public world, where they could privately make music for the consumption of millions. The group spent an unprecedented five months making *Sgt Pepper's Lonely Hearts Club Band*, issued in June 1967 to massive acclaim. But less than three months after its release, at the apex of their musical career, the Beatles were deeply shocked by the death of their manager Brian Epstein. John's immediate yet private reaction – unveiled to Jann Wenner of *Rolling Stone* in 1970 – was succinct and typically Lennon, 'I thought, we've fucking had it'.

Though Epstein's influence over the Beatles had grown more tenuous as the 1960s progressed, it can be no coincidence that their first major public failure with the TV film *Magical Mystery Tour*, the naive setting-up of their Apple group of companies, and the sudden disharmony between John, Paul, George and Ringo, all occurred within months of his death. Even the recording studio, where they were usually comfortable, stretched their tolerance to breaking point. Tempers frayed badly during summer 1968 sessions for their double 'White Album' – *The Beatles* – and Ringo actually quit the group, albeit temporarily and amid great secrecy. 'They were getting very tense in the studio and were arguing amongst themselves,' remembers their recording engineer Geoff Emerick. 'They really wanted to get out of the studio ... they probably couldn't see the light at the end of the tunnel. It was just messy recording, they'd deliberately play where they weren't supposed to play, to make the job harder than it really was.'

Though the bad reaction to *Magical Mystery Tour* had shown that, at last, the media were examining the Beatles without rose-tinted spectacles, Beatlemania and the old stereotyped roles still surfaced from time to time. In July 1968, while recording the 'White Album', their animated film *Yellow Submarine* was premiered. Sanctioned by the group in 1967 but played-down by them ever after, it reflected the optimistic, psychedelic mood of the previous summer, when music and love would save the world, and it further underlined the outmoded Fab Four character roles set four years earlier by Alun Owen.

But the summer of 1968 was no time for peace, bells and love, love, love. It was a time of street demonstrations in Paris, Prague and London. And by now John was deeply involved in his relationship with Yoko Ono, and with her support was actively seeking to break away from the cartoon caricature of Beatledom.

In keeping with his now earnest efforts to strip away the façade of the Beatles, to 'smash the myth' as he put it, John was anxious to shed any gloss. When the group began the *Get Back* project in January 1969, which developed into *Let It Be*, the Beatles actually said that they wanted to be seen 'warts and all', or 'as nature intended' to quote press advertisements for the 'Get Back' single in April 1969. They allowed cameras to film their rehearsals for a new LP, which began only eleven weeks after the exhausting and tense 'White Album' had been completed.

As director Michael Lindsay-Hogg recalls, 'One day, when we went up for lunch, George came up and said, "I'll see you around the clubs" and he left, and that was that. They thought it was goodbye for ever, and John, with his usual mixture of pragmatism and brutality, said, "Let's call Eric Clapton and get him". Then, when we went back on to the stage again, Yoko sat on George's blue cushion. It was a very symbolic gesture.' But like Ringo before him, George Harrison was persuaded to rejoin the group soon after quitting.

Six months later, while making their final album *Abbey Road*, the Beatles previewed the first rough cut of *Get Back* – a print which was significantly different to the released version. 'About a day or two later I got a call from Peter Brown [an Apple executive],' recalls Lindsay-Hogg. 'He said, "How can I put it? I've had three phone calls this morning and I think quite a lot of the stuff with John and Yoko should come out" ... I think the others were slightly fed up with John and Yoko as a couple, influencing the Beatles.'

Soon after beginning their relationship in May 1968 it had become obvious to John that, in Yoko, he had found a partner capable of filling any void left by ending the Beatles. Ironically though, it was Paul McCartney – who had tried more than anyone to keep the group intact – who finally split the group with an announcement in April 1970.

'It's just natural,' John told the BBC in 1971. 'It's not a great disaster. People keep talking about it as if it's the end of the earth. It's only a rock group that's split up! It's nothing important! It's like a rugby team – sometime you have to get married and leave the boys on a Saturday night. And that's how it is.'

THE BEATLES
"LET IT BE" U
TECHNICOLOR ®
UNITED ARTISTS

Without gloss,
the Beatles and Yoko 'as nature intended'
during *Let It Be*

In His Own Write And Draw

John Lennon's book *In His Own Write* was published at the end of March 1964, just a month after the Beatles' return from their first 'invasion' of the United States. This was the trip in which Beatlemania had swamped the American market with a wave of hysteria generated by the group's 'mop-top' looks, mildly irreverent repartee and, of course, fresh and youthful music. Songs like 'From Me To You', 'She Loves You' and 'I Want To Hold Your Hand' had words which continued the variation on popular music's favourite themes of boy meets girl or boy loses girl. They had charm and were perfect for the musical style of the records but had no ambition to be anything other than direct, personal and catchy.

Most readers of *In His Own Write*, whether Beatles' fans or literary critics, would have been surprised by its content. It was hard to reconcile John's expression of such beautifully simple thoughts as 'When I touch you I feel happy inside', with his writing about 'Partly Dave' who 'lept off the bus like a burning spastic'. It was easy enough to trace the roots of John's words and music with the Beatles, but more perplexing to be confronted by the bizarre word-play and subject matter

> *'I had one mind that wrote books or funny stories and another mind that churned out things about "I love you" and "You love me", 'cause that is how Paul and I did it ... I suddenly realised, I'll use all that energy on the song, forget about* In His Own Write *and put it all in the song.'*
>
> JOHN LENNON

of his first book.

In fact, John's literary roots were planted firmly in his childhood. 'You always found Mimi tucked into a book,' recalls John's step-sister Julia Baird. 'She's an intensive reader. As children, we all read under the bedclothes, with torches, and were all told that we'd go short-sighted – and nearly all of us did! John would read *anything*, he read avidly.' Having learnt to share his Aunt's literary appetite, as a youngster John liked to amuse his family and friends with his own witty writings and drawings. Julia was delighted by the books he created with 'Cartoon characters and balloons coming out saying "Wow!". Once he drew me a dinosaur and the girl in the next road said "That's too good for you" and I said "Yes, I know, John did it". So he did about thirty more then!'

John would later recall how he craved recognition for his precocious writing and drawing talents. In a bitter interview with *Rolling Stone* magazine's Jann Wenner in 1970 he spoke of the frustration of being aware of his 'genius, so-called, at ten, eight, nine. I always thought ... why has nobody discovered me?' and he accused his Aunt Mimi of neglecting his intellect by throwing out his poetry – rather

A TREASURY OF
ART and POETRY

This book contains only the work of J.W.Lennon, with additional work by J.W.Lennon, and a helping hand given by J.W.Lennon, not forgetting J.W.Lennon.
Who is this J.W.Lennon?
Here are some remark by a few famous Newspapers.

"A good book better"—J.W.Lennon of the Daily Howl
"This book has many good uses and should go down well" — The Sanitory Journal
"Yes" — Freo Emney Fan Club Magazine
"(Belch!)" — Garston Herald.

"And then there's the one about the Bishop and the actress....."

unfairly as some early examples of his work were preserved. The artwork of the 1974 album *Walls And Bridges* duly featured paintings by 'John W Lennon Age 11', given back to him by Mimi.

During his years at Quarry Bank High School, John shaped his childhood drawings into cruel caricatures of masters and classmates often featured in his hand-written comic book the *Daily Howl* which was furtively passed around the school. He was a rebellious pupil who defied authority and conventional education, although he did acknowledge the encouragement of an English teacher, Philip Burnett, who noticed his unusual writing talent. With the help of headmaster William Pobjoy, John was admitted to Liverpool College of Art purely on the strength of his portfolio of art work, having failed all his GCE 'O' Levels.

He attended art school for three years from September 1957 and found that the unconventional view of life reflected in his cartoons and poetry could be shared with students like Stuart Sutcliffe, Rod Murray and Bill Harry. Eventually, Bill was the first to publish John's pieces and he remembers being excited by their originality and Englishness during an era of strong influence from American 'Beat Generation' poets like Ginsberg, Corso and Ferlinghetti. 'I heard that John wrote poetry ... and I asked him if he had an example. He was embarrassed at first ... I got the impression that he felt that writing poetry was a bit effeminate because he had this tough macho image. But I said "I'm genuinely interested". So he showed me a poem and I thought it was very good. It was a rustic poem, it was pure British humour and comedy, and I loved it'.

Bill Harry recognised a similarity to the 'fractured English' of Stanley Unwin, whom John would have heard on the radio in the late fifties. Combined with this 'gobbledegook' style of word play was the mark of the fantastic imagery in Lewis Carroll's 'Alice' books which John loved as a child. When Bill started his influential music paper *Mersey Beat*, he included in the first issue, published in July 1961, a typical piece of literary Lennon entitled 'On The Dubious Origins of Beatles'.

Many people ask what are Beatles? Why Beatles? Ugh, Beatles, how did the name arrive? So we will tell you. It came in a vision – a man appeared on a flaming pie and said unto them 'From this day on you are Beatles with an A'. Thank you, Mister Man, they said, thanking him.

Filled with the confidence of seeing his bizarre history of the group in print, John gave Bill Harry a large number of his drawings, stories and poems for publication in *Mersey Beat*. Every so often his writings would appear under the 'Beatcomber' heading, a pun on the humorous *Daily Express* column 'Beachcomber'. As the Beatles' career gathered speed and their popularity could no longer be contained on Merseyside alone, John continued to scribble down his thoughts and jottings. Towards the end of 1963, with all of Britain consumed by Beatlemania, the idea grew that John's work might be enjoyed by a wider readership than *Mersey Beat* and his close circle of friends.

In a 1965 BBC-TV interview with Kenneth Allsop, John admitted that if he had not been famous his work might have remained unpublished. 'I would have been crawling around broke and just writing it and throwing it away,' he revealed, adding that it was Michael Braun, the author of *Love Me Do* – an account of the group in the throes of British Beatlemania – who introduced his work to a publisher. Jonathan Cape was delighted to be able to publish *In His Own Write*, the first literary endeavour of a Beatle. It was a best-seller, with sales of 100 000 in its first printing, and the media fell in love with the notion of an intelligent book-writing pop star – an unprecedented diversion from the music business stereotype of an incoherently mumbling illiterate.

John's book was a frequent topic for Beatles interviews, and the other three played along and generally made fun of it. On the *Public Ear* radio programme broadcast on 22 March 1964, George Harrison adopted the role of a 'posh' BBC interviewer to talk about *In His Own Write*.

'It's a laugh-a-minute with John Lennon. Some of you might have found it a bit difficult to understand because, you see, it's in a sort of funny lingo ... I don't really know how you could describe it but it's sort of rubbish! Maybe that's one way.'

At the end of the 'interview', John read 'Alec Speaking' – a prime example of his playful nonsensical word play:

Strab he down the soddieflays
Amo amat amass;
Amonk amink a minibus,
Amarmylaidie Moon,
Amikky mendip multiplus
Amighty midgey spoon.

John's amusement at the absurdities of life was reflected through his poetry, prose and line drawings. Amongst the characters were 'The Moldy Moldy Man', 'Henry and Harry' who were born to be 'Brummer Strivers', 'Sad Michael', who was 'debb and duff and could not speeg', and 'Good Dog Nigel'.

Nice dog! Goo boy,
Waggie tail and beg,
Clever Nigel, jump for joy
Because we're putting you to sleep at three of the clock, Nigel.

Soon after the publication of *In His Own Write*, Christina Foyle, founder of the famous London bookstore, threw a grand luncheon in John's honour at the plush Dorchester Hotel. The highlight was to be John's speech, but apparently hung-over and among company he perhaps would not have chosen himself, he shocked the expectant guests with the briefest address ever recorded at such an event: 'Er, thank you very much. God bless you!' Beatles' manager Brian Epstein came to the rescue and gave a longer, more considered response to the disappointed diners. John later explained to a BBC reporter that he had simply been too 'scared stiff' to attempt a speech.

Despite the Gala Luncheon and the book topping the best-sellers lists, not everyone was so ecstatic about *In His Own Write*. Speaking in the House of Commons on 19 June 1964, Mr Charles Curran, Conservative MP for Uxbridge, feared for the literacy of the nation. At a time when the whole world seemed to be buzzing with Beatlemania, he admitted he'd 'never seen or heard the Beatles' but had been interested to read John's book. He quoted for the House verses from 'Deaf Ted, Danoota, (and me)'

Thorg Billy grows and Burnley ten,
And Aston Villa three
We clobber ever gallup
Deaf Ted, Danoota and me.

So if you hear a wonderous sight,
Am blutter or at sea,
Remember whom the mighty say
Deaf Ted, Danoota, and me.

Mr Curran concluded that John 'has a feeling for words and story-telling but he is in a state of pathetic near-literacy' and felt that more academic schooling was needed in the future for pupils of similar potential.

If the MP had missed the humour and delight with words displayed in John's work, the literary critics had not. *The Times Literary Supplement* recommended the book for 'anyone who fears for the impoverishment of the English Language and British imagination'. When his second book *A Spaniard In The Works* was published in June 1965, John once more found himself feted by the literary world and in alien territory for a pop star. He was featured on the BBC Home Service programme *World of Books* with Wilfred De'Ath, who flattered John with an earnest examination of the Lennon literary style.

The interview was both funny and revealing. Questioned on the influences that critics saw in his work, John would admit only to Lewis Carroll. 'I bought all the books that they said it was like ... one book on Edward Lear, *Finnegan's Wake* [by James Joyce], a big book on Chaucer and I couldn't see any resemblance to any of them. [Perhaps] a little bit of *Finnegan's Wake* but [that] was so way-out and so different, just a few word changes, but anybody who changes words is going to be compared.'

Asked whether the use of a technical device like onomatopoeia was contrived, John had to be given an explanation of what it was.

Lennon: That's three words I've learnt today!

De'Ath: You know when I say a word like 'buzz', 'buzz' is an onomatopoeia because in the word is captured the noise of the bee ... and you probably without realising it ... your book is full of them.

Lennon: Is it? Well, I'm glad to know that. Lot of onomatopoeias ... I just haven't a clue what you're talking about really. Automatic pier, sounds like to me. That's probably why I change words, 'cause I haven't a clue what words mean half the time.

John also explained that although his work was very spontaneous, and rarely revised, the writing of his second book had demanded a more disciplined approach than the first because, with a publishing deadline, he had to 'start from scratch ... in the first book, a lot of it I'd written at odd times during my life'.

A Spaniard In The Works, like his first book, was peopled with characters whose deformities, disabilities, even colour or creed, were mercilessly lampooned. In the title piece, 'Jesus El Pifco was a foreigner and he knew it ... a garlic eating, stinking, little yellow greasy fascist bastard catholic Spaniard.' In another, 'Our Dad' is kicked out of his home by his sons

'You don't want me around,' he said,
'I'm old and crippled too.'
We didn't have the heart to say
'You're bloody right it's true.'

The grotesque drawings in the book were equally funny and cruel. A street busker with a sign declaring 'I Am Blind' stands next to another with a placard reading 'I Can See Quite Clearly'. When asked about his so called 'sick' humour, John linked it back to his school days: 'We used to draw a lot and pass it round and I remember we had some blind dogs with sunglasses on leading ordinary people ... a lot of gags like that at school'.

Art school friend Bill Harry had also

De'Ath: 'A lot of people say your pieces are sick. What do you say to them?'
Lennon: 'If it makes people sick, they're sick. It doesn't appear sick to me'

encountered this characteristic during word association games when John 'would come out with things like "spastic" or "cripple" and seemed obsessed with this. But people may not understand this was at the peak of what was called the "sick joke" period.' It was a type of humour the Beatles shared, but John would go further, mocking taboo subjects publicly, even mimicking spastic movements onstage at Beatles' concerts.

A Spaniard In The Works was John's last collection of new writing published during his lifetime. By mid-1965 he began to realise that his word play and sense of the surreal could be incorporated into his songs rather than on to the printed page. It was the example of new literate song-writers of that time, particularly Bob Dylan, which demonstrated that the record-buying public would accept a more sophisticated use of words in pop music, and Dylan's album *Bringing It All Back Home*, released in the spring of 1965, was the trail-blazer. Hearing Dylan's songs with a rock backing for the first time was like listening to Baudelaire sung by Chuck Berry. The album topped the British chart and spawned a remarkable hit single 'Sub-terranean Homesick Blues'. With its playful use of words – 'Maggie comes fleet foot, face full of black soot' – it struck a chord with John.

This impact on John's lyric writing was first noticeable on the Beatles' album *Rubber Soul* released at the end of 1965. 'Norwegian Wood (This Bird has Flown)' told the story of an adulterous affair, but was veiled in poetic imagery and *double entendre*. Indeed the opening lines 'I once had a girl, or should I say she once had me' had at least *three* meanings. 'Nowhere Man' and 'In My Life' were introspective and reflective, the first questioning John's role as an artist within the strictures of being a Beatle; the second, an aching look

back to his pre-fame years, 'The first time I consciously put the literary part of myself into the lyric', he later said. In 1966 he wrote 'Strawberry Fields Forever', which hauntingly evoked the innocence of child-hood but also, a sense of isolation through seeing the world differently, 'No one, I think, is in my tree'. The song was recorded during sessions for the first album after the Beatles stopped touring and at a time when the group were heavily influenced by the hallucinogenic drug LSD.

On *Sgt Pepper's Lonely Hearts Club Band*, John's graphic imagination was given full rein, his song 'Lucy In The Sky With Diamonds' clearly showing that the two writing minds he had talked of were now focused as one. The 'Marmalade Skies' brought to mind the 'Amarmylaidie Moon' of 'Alec Speaking', and there was the coupling of words like 'looking-glass ties' and 'plasticine porters' purely for the pleasure of the sound they made. Critics and fans revelled in the search for secret messages of enlightenment that might be concealed within and could not resist seeing the letters LSD looming large in the title 'Lucy In The Sky With Diamonds'.

With hindsight, it seems that Lewis Carroll was much more of an influence on John's work than LSD, the poem 'The Walrus And The Carpenter' inspiring the title of another classic of 1967 psychedelia 'I Am The Walrus'. Here the imagery was more menacing than in 'Lucy In The Sky With Diamonds' – 'Yellow matter custard dripping from a dead dog's eye' – was worthy of the cinema's arch-surrealist Luis Buñuel. For the first time in a song, John invented words: *'Crabalocker* fish-wife', 'expert *texpert*', and the recurring refrain *'Goo Goo G'Joob'*. For anyone seeking meaning in this glorious jumble of images, John was not helpful. ' "I am the eggman" ... could have been the pudding basin for all I care. It's just tongue-in-

John with Victor Spinetti on the BBC-TV programme *Release*, 22 June 1968, discussing the one-act play adapted from his books

'Where's your wife then, John?' For the first time, Yoko Ono steps into the glare of publicity generated by a Beatle at the National Theatre, 18 June 1968

cheek. It's not that serious.'

At the end of 1967, while 'I Am The Walrus' nestled at the top of the charts on the flipside of Paul McCartney's rather more straightforward 'Hello, Goodbye', John was asked to work on an adaptation of his two books for Sir Laurence Olivier's National Theatre. His friend Victor Spinetti, a veteran of three Beatles' films, was asked to direct and co-write the piece as a one act play. He recalls, 'I remember sitting one day in the flat and John suddenly said "Hey Vic, let's go somewhere warmer". I thought he meant another room – we ended up in Africa!' Spinetti marvelled at John's 'most amazing facility for words' and the speed at which he could write. 'I said to him we need a speech here – a Queen's ship-launching speech for the character to say as he stands on his bed and is going to launch out into the world – he wrote, instantly, "My housebound and eyeball take great pressure in denouncing this ship ..." Aside from the fact that the Chaucerian word for husband is "housebound", it was straight, direct and a marvellous opening line.'

In a BBC-TV interview in June 1968, John acknowledged that through the dramatisation of his books, Spinetti had uncovered a submerged core of meaning. 'When I saw the rehearsal, I felt quite emotional ... I was too involved with it when it was written ... it took something like this to make me see what I was about then.' The theme of the play was remembrance of times past: the first impressions of going to the theatre, watching television, the cinema, the first book, the first date. As Victor recalled, John said that he had been made to 'think of all the things I used to think about when I was sixteen'. It was a central theme in John's life and work for many more years to come.

The National Theatre production called *In His Own Write* opened on 18 June 1968 and John attended the first night with Japanese avant-garde artist Yoko Ono, prompting photographers to shout rudely, 'Where's your wife then, John?' In fact, John had begun his relationship with Yoko the previous month when, as Victor Spinetti puts it, he had found 'a great playmate'. Yoko's radically original ideas and behaviour had impressed John since the end of 1966 when he had attended one of her conceptual art shows at the Indica Gallery in London. He was also intrigued by her book *Grapefruit*, full of imaginary 'pieces' with tantalising titles like 'Painting To Be Constructed In Your Head.' John and Yoko recognised in each other's work a child-like quality which was refreshingly anti-intellectual. At the end of 1968 the Beatles' 'White Album' was released, featuring a fine example of John's playfulness with words. 'Happiness Is A Warm Gun' revisited similar terrain to 'Walrus', with 'multicoloured mirrors' on hobnail boots and the line 'A soap impression of his wife which he ate and donated to the National Trust'. 'Across The Universe', recorded around this time, was a more gentle and seductive dip into poetry with a pleasing parade of elemental images: 'waves of joy', 'restless wind' and the shining of 'a million suns'.

But as John plunged into a bewildering array of projects with Yoko – sound collage albums, avant-garde films, concerts, exhibitions and events for peace – his lyric writing began to take another direction. Their peace campaign taught John that simplicity made for directness. 'Give Peace A Chance' and the follow-up Plastic Ono Band single 'Cold Turkey' were straightforward messages forcefully delivered and easily understood. During 1969, John's songwriting started to shed surreal imagery and the following year it returned to the basic expression of feeling.

'At school we used to draw a lot and pass it round and I remember we had blind dogs with sunglasses on leading ordinary people.' Aged thirty, John's drawing still continued the schoolboy theme

Made after the Beatles' break-up, the album *John Lennon/Plastic Ono Band* stood in stark contrast to what he described as his 'Dylanesque' songs. John often referred to it as the 'Mother' album and that opening song's bluntness – 'Mother, you had me, But I never had you' – crystallised the new approach.

The posthumous publication in 1986 of the collection *Skywriting By Word Of Mouth* demonstrated that John later returned to playing with words on paper, especially in his 'house-husband' period, during his five-year absence from recording. His prose also had the irreverence of his sixties books with lines like 'Yea, tho' I walk thru Rudy Vallee, I will fear no Evel Knievel'. But his seventies' songs stayed true to the spirit of the 'Mother' album.

In one of his last interviews, in December 1980, John Lennon told the BBC's Andy Peebles that he had wanted to 'shave off all imagery, pretensions of poetry ... just say what it is, simple English, make it rhyme and put a back-beat on it and express yourself as simply and straightforwardly as possible. [But] I enjoy the poetic side and I'll probably do a little dabble later ...'

Tomorrow Never Knows

John Lennon was enchanted by the recording process. He was always a 'record man', and in his own work, strove to capture on tape the emotional 'feel' of a studio performance combined with an inventive musical arrangement and sound.

From 1966, the Beatles, with their producer George Martin and engineer Geoff Emerick, pushed aside the barriers of music recording. Their discs heralded an era of enormous and quite unforeseen change in rock music, and the new studio techniques and trickery they employed typified the group's – and John's – perpetual experimentation and quest for new sounds.

However, in 1962, when the Beatles cut their first single, the whole principle of recording had been entirely different. Producer George Martin recalls that the aim then was to make a record as faithfully true to the original performance as possible. 'It would be like a photograph and nobody ever deviated from that. They used to do experiments where they would have loudspeakers and orchestras playing behind curtains and say "Which one is the orchestra and which one is the tape?" '

When this recording technique was applied to British pop music it yielded

> *'We got knowledge of the studio. If I go in there and just sing and play ... as soon as someone tells me we can get a little reverb on it, or if I stand over there, it'll sound different than if I stand here, then I begin to start learning ...'*
>
> JOHN LENNON

disappointing results for musicians trying to emulate the authentic sound of American rock and roll. In 1973, John spoke to the BBC about the problems that groups like the Beatles had encountered in the early sixties. 'The fact was, there hadn't been a history of making that kind of music, whereas there had in America. You had to fight that thing about the needle going into the red, which is bullshit, to try to get the volume on to the record.'

The early Beatles' sessions adhered to two basic principles. First, capture the group pretty much as they sounded live; and second, do it quickly and economically. Hence, all ten new tracks for the group's first album *Please Please Me* were taped in a single day, 11 February 1963. George Martin recalls, 'That was opportunism really. I needed an album very quickly and what easier way than to put up a microphone and say "Sing in front of that, lads!" ' With only a minor degree of overdubbing of voices and instruments, *Please Please Me* demonstrates how exciting and proficient the Beatles were as a live band.

From 1963 to 1965, the group's recording sessions were squeezed into a whirlwind schedule whipped up by the spread of Beatlemania, and although subsequent albums did take longer than a single day, they were still done in days rather than weeks. Remarkably, two Beatles' albums were delivered each year during that time, in addition to more new material being issued on singles. At the end of 1965, the album *Rubber Soul* signified that their recordings were becoming more unconventional. The treatment of sound through equalisation – the 'toppy' guitars of 'Nowhere Man', the distorted fuzz-bass of 'Think For Yourself' – were clearly departures from the principle of faithful recording. But the full revolution in the studio came with *Revolver* released in August 1966.

The Beatles began work on this album with a new engineer. Through to *Rubber Soul*, Norman Smith had balanced their records. After promotion to EMI's A&R department he was replaced by twenty-year-old Geoff Emerick, a maverick keen to join the group in tearing up the recording rule book. 'In those days EMI drastically filtered out the bass content in case any records jumped,' he says. 'But, anyway, I proceeded to record bass drums with the mike a lot closer and then got a letter from the management saying that you weren't allowed to go nearer than a foot, but they'd give special permission in this circumstance. They used to throw their hands up in horror!'

In the institutional and rather straight-laced atmosphere of EMI, the Beatles were also fortunate to be coupled with a producer who had proved his willingness to experiment with sound recording. George Martin had produced records by the likes of Peter Sellers, Spike Milligan, and the Temperance Seven, chock full of comic effects and tape trickery. He had collaborated with the BBC's experimental Radiophonic Workshop on a record by 'Ray Cathode' which featured the weird and wonderful distortion of recorded sound. George Martin did not have a rock background, but he had an open mind, and open ears, to the pursuit of the unorthodox.

John described the creative partnership between the Beatles and George Martin to the BBC's Bob Harris in 1975: 'He had a very great musical knowledge and background, so he could translate for us and suggest a lot of amazing technical things ... we'd be saying we want it to go "Ooh-ooh!" and "Ee-ee!" and he'd say, "Well, look chaps, I thought of this ..." and we'd say "Oh, great! Great! Put it on here!" It's hard to say who did what ... he taught us a lot and I'm sure we taught him a lot by our primitive musical ability.'

The sessions for *Revolver* began in April 1966 with 'Tomorrow Never Knows', a recording overflowing with innovative studio techniques. First, the sound of John's voice was electronically altered. From their earliest sessions, the Beatles had used the technique of 'double tracking', where the lead singer would overdub a new vocal along with his original track, adding texture to the quality of his voice. It was a tricky and time-consuming chore which John, whose studio work was usually governed by impatience, hoped might be achieved more easily. 'Artificial Double Tracking', devised by EMI's Ken Townsend, was the solution. The original recording of a voice was put back into the mix slightly delayed, giving the illusion of two voices. Nowadays, ADT is achieved through the use of digital delay, but in the mid-sixties a rather unwieldy contraption, with a large lever, was used, and the few milliseconds of delay were made by vari-speeding a tape machine. John loved the effect and affectionately nicknamed ADT 'flanging' or 'phasing', words still in use today.

Top George Martin listens to John running through a song at EMI's studios in Abbey Road on 1 July 1963, the day the Beatles recorded 'She Loves You' and its B-Side 'I'll Get You'. Their producer's primary function at this stage was to help with the structure and arrangement of the songs

Bottom John Lennon was always enchanted by the recording process

On 'Tomorrow Never Knows', John's vocal was further influenced by a desire for an atmospheric sound to match his boundless imagination. George Martin remembers that John wanted 'to sound like a Dalai Lama singing from a hilltop.' Rather than get on the next plane to Tibet, the solution was to feed John's voice through a rotating speaker (the Leslie speaker used with a Hammond organ). The resulting vibrato effect enthralled John and the other Beatles and led to their putting guitars, drums and piano through the Leslie. As Geoff Emerick wryly remembers, 'It got to the point where John said, "Get some rope, suspend me from the ceiling of the studio and swing me around the mike while I sing!" Somehow, we never quite got around to that particular idea . . .'

The urge to alter the sound of his voice artificially was a constant feature of John's recording career. 'I thought he had a wonderful voice', says George Martin. 'But he hated it, so I had to do things to it that would intrigue him and turn him on.'

Yet another of the elements in 'Tomorrow Never Knows' was the use of strange ethereal noises, created by tape loops. Paul McCartney had developed the idea by unhooking the erase head of his Brennell tape machine at home, which allowed a sound to be recorded over and over again, saturating the tape. The others were impressed, manufactured their own loops and took them into the Abbey Road studio where they were played from machines all around the building and injected into the control desk. With eight loops running all the time, the sounds were mixed 'live' over the music, with the desk used like a musical instrument. 'I played the faders like a modern day synthesiser,' says Geoff Emerick.

Thereafter, the manipulation of sound by tape trickery became a feature of Beatles' recordings. Just a week after work had begun on the epic 'Tomorrow Never Knows', another new sound entered the repertoire, backwards taping. 'Rain' is the first Beatles track to feature a backwards sound. George Martin, 'always wanting to please the boys', dubbed off a section of John's vocal, turned the tape around and played it over the end of the song. 'He flipped! He thought it was absolutely fantastic, it was like a Russian sound with all the consonants backwards and it gave a dream-like feel to the song, which, I guess, is why John liked it so much. He was always a dreamer.' The trance-like mood of another of John's *Revolver* tracks, 'I'm Only Sleeping', is also enhanced by evocative backwards electric guitars.

As the Beatles' increasingly sophisticated songs were developing in the studio, so their work soared to a creative peak. Geoff Emerick's artistic role was to 'paint a picture with tones and sounds. John would say "Give me an orange sound", and you could tell by his face or his mood whether he was happy with that sound. There wasn't a lot of verbal communication.'

After ending the numbing monotony of concert touring in August 1966, the Beatles essentially became a studio group and pursued their pioneering methods of recording ever more thoroughly. The sessions for their next LP, *Sgt Pepper's Lonely Hearts Club Band*, began with a song, eventually left off the album, which hazily conjured up the childhood memory of rambling in the grounds of a Salvation Army hostel near where John had lived. His 'Strawberry Fields Forever' is a monumental recording, encapsulating the Beatles' experimentation of the previous year: the use of backwards tapes, electronic vocal treatment, and orchestral instruments in a rock context. The track also

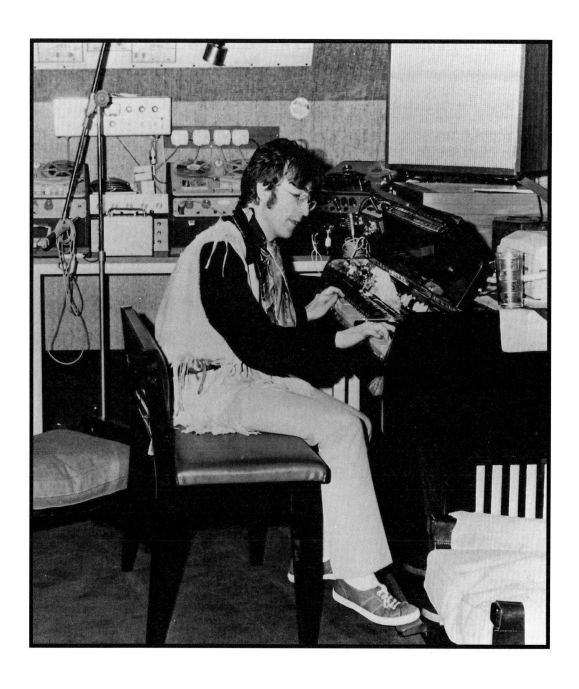

John in 1967 at his home studio in Weybridge, Surrey. His and Yoko's first work together, *Two Virgins*, was recorded here in May 1968

featured an early appearance of the mellotron – a clumsy precursor to modern day sampling keyboards – from which, at the press of a key, the sound of various instruments recorded on loops of tape could be produced.

The master-take of 'Strawberry Fields Forever' was completed because of John's belief that anything was possible in a recording studio, given the right ideas and talented people to carry them out. The Beatles recorded two quite distinct versions of the song. The first, a gentle rendition, with electric guitar and mellotron to the fore, and the second, more agitated and tense, scored by George Martin for trumpets and cellos. Faced with choosing between them, John opted instead for the first part of the earlier electric version to be combined with the later scored one. Even the calm George Martin was disturbed by such a request.

'I said, "Well, the only problem is they're in different keys and different tempos". And he said, "Yeah, but you can fix it." It never occurred to him that there would be any difficulties. He was never concerned with technicalities, in John's mind it was very rational, he believed that people could do magical things without being questioned. I swore under my breath and then thought about it a great deal and worked it out. God was on our side.'

By speeding up the slower electric version and dropping down the faster orchestral version, Martin found a point where both the tempos and keys could be matched. The edit worked and the two different interpretations were combined into one astounding record, 'Strawberry Fields Forever'. It was released as a single in February 1967, with Paul McCartney's own Liverpool evocation, 'Penny Lane', on the other side. Four months later came the release of the *Sgt Pepper* album, heralded by many as the apogee of the creative collaboration between all four Beatles and their producer and engineers.

Working for George Martin during this time was Tony King, who remembers Beatles' sessions being 'like all the fun of the fair. Everybody would have those funny sort of sixties' smiles on their faces. And amongst all this madness there was the Duke of Edinburgh, as we used to call George Martin.' Tony observed how John's wildest ideas would be rationally interpreted and given life by his producer. 'Like in "I Am The Walrus" those wonderful "Goo Goo G'Joob" sounds were sung by the Mike Sammes Singers and it was all very written out and orchestrated.' The surreal imagery of 'I Am The Walrus' was brilliantly conveyed in a bizarre cacophony of sound. Released only four years after 'She Loves You', it displayed an entirely different approach to music, mixing a rock rhythm track with strings, sound effects and even a live radio feed of a BBC broadcast of Shakespeare's *The Tragedy Of King Lear*.

However, as the heady year of 1967 drew to a close, John began to grow disenchanted with the artifice used on 'Walrus' and *Sgt Pepper*. For him, the pop album's new elevated status as an individual art form was a betrayal of the music's earthy rock and roll roots, and in 1968 he separated his experiments with sound from his music making. The catalyst for this change was Yoko Ono, 'I realised somebody else was as barmy as me,' John recalled in 1980.

Their relationship began in May 1968 when they worked on a collage recording in John's home studio in Weybridge, Surrey. That night's dabblings were released the following November on the album *Two Virgins*. It was an uncompromising clash of two cultures: John's northern English music-hall humour set against Yoko's New York free-form dissonance. They later released two other, similar collaborations, *Life With The Lions* and *Wedding Album*, neither seeking nor finding widespread public acclaim.

Two Virgins led directly to the Beatles and George Martin making a collage for the 'White Album', and via 'Revolution 9' the avant-garde world was introduced to the mass record-buying public for the first time. John described the track as 'the most important Beatle music made in the last four years'. Once more, George Martin was enthusiastic about a radical move. 'You could sit in front of those two speakers and actually see things happening if you shut your eyes. It wasn't music but it was a sound picture. I love "Revolution 9".'

During 1968 and 1969, the Beatles remained at the forefront of the rock revolution cutting edge as they experimented with new recording technology such as the prototype Moog synthesiser. However, alongside the studio experimentation there was also a noticeable return to the capturing of real performances that might be duplicated onstage. Indeed, the tracks for *Let It Be*, recorded in January 1969, were originally intended to have no production embellishment at all, and simply be a documentary record of how the group sounded live, without overdubbing or technical trickery. But when Phil Spector was later brought in to 're-produce' the tapes, the end result veered well away from that principle.

John began his career as a solo artist in 1969 too, and his work without the other Beatles was recorded differently. Surrounded by a variety of musicians and producers, he went through a range of recording styles: from the busker-like ambiance of 'Give Peace A Chance', to the raw, bare intensity of 'Cold Turkey' and to the thumping echo-laden 'Instant Karma!'.

The production of his first two solo albums of the seventies – *John Lennon/Plastic Ono Band* and *Imagine* – was shared by John and Yoko with the creator of the legendary 'Wall of Sound', Phil Spector. Aside from the American's trademark of heavy echo, the albums are free of Spector's usual production hallmarks. Rather than the overwhelming force of a 'rock orchestra', *John Lennon/Plastic Ono Band* has, in sharp contrast, minimalist instrumentation of piano, guitar, bass and drums. The intimacy of that sound combined with soul-searching lyrics and powerful performances deliver a forceful blow to the senses. It remains a timeless masterpiece.

Imagine had a more augmented sound with 'sweetening' string overdubs added to tracks laid down by a nucleus of musicians at John's home studio at Tittenhurst Park in Ascot. He relished the opportunity to direct and motivate top musicians, enforcing a schedule of two recordings a night, the basic tracks for the album were completed within a week.

Ace keyboard player Nicky Hopkins fondly remembers the atmosphere at the *Imagine* sessions of July 1971. 'They had the "apparency" of being somewhat laid back and yet, at the same time, there was a tight control on it. It's the funniest thing because John was able to get things done very quickly but with no sacrifice at all to quality and without any bullying. Once, when one of the sax players opened his case, pulled out a bag of "grass" and was gonna roll up a number, John said, "Could we leave that till after the session? Then we can all sit back and relax. In the meantime, if we can just get on with it or else we'll all forget where we are." '

With the exception of the anarchic sessions for the *Rock 'n' Roll* album, when John surrendered the production role entirely to Phil Spector, this dedicated approach in the studio was constant throughout the remainder of his solo recordings. Working on the 1974 album *Walls And Bridges* was a young engineer, and now top producer, Jimmy Iovine, who still regards the sessions as '*The* most professional I have ever been on. John was going after a noise and he knew how to get it. His solo work had an incredible sound to it but it didn't sound like the Beatles, it really sounded like him.'

Integral to the production was the special treatment of John's voice. For a track like ' #9 Dream', balance engineer Roy Cicala would contrive a vocal sound which had echo, tape-delay reverberation and double-tracking mixed into it.

The insecurity about his voice which George Martin first noted in the sixties stayed with John throughout his career. Prior to recording the 1980 album *Double Fantasy*, co-producer Jack Douglas received primitive demo cassettes, and even on these John had gone to great pains to double-track his vocal.

'No one could ever tell him he had the best rock and roll voice in the world,' Jack laughs, adding that he was also made aware of John's need to record quickly. 'He could lose his patience with a piece of equipment if it was laying him up for a while. He would go mad. There was never a lull; there was never a wasted moment.' Although John had kept away from professional recording during his 'house-husband' period from 1975 to 1980 – a time of rapid studio development – it did not take him long to feel at home when he turned his attention to it again. His musical creativity was once more focused on the studio, where he was both an inspired and efficient artist.

The craftsmanship of John's best solo tracks demonstrated his skill when directing musicians and his experimental work in the sixties with the Beatles has helped redefine the entire philosophy of rock and pop music recording. As a 'studio animal' John was able to escape any pressures on him there and enjoy the opportunity to capture a magical moment on tape. Jimmy Iovine remembers being astonished when, during Lennon's 1974 'Green Card' battles to stay in the United States, he 'would come back, wearing a suit from being in court and sing like he'd never been there … he was so natural at it. God, was he tremendous.'

Though his peers remain hugely impressed by John's achievements in the studio, George Martin was to discover that, even in this area of his life, John restlessly searched for something that remained forever unattainable.

'We were chatting about old times and he suddenly said to me "Do you know, George, if I could have my time all over again, I'd record every one of those tracks again. I don't think any of them were any good". That completely floored me. He always had that elusive ideal that he never actually captured. Dreams are so fragile and life is so hard that in reality dreams cannot be for real. But John always wanted them to be.'

Top At the studio control desk in his Tittenhurst Park
home near Ascot, where most of *Imagine* was recorded
Bottom Five-year-old Sean receives a lesson in modern
recording at New York's Hit Factory

Two Of Us

John Lennon and Paul McCartney – popular music's premier songwriting partnership – have already secured their place in the cultural history of the twentieth century as the creators of scores of immortal songs, and as the driving force within the Beatles. Their names are, even now, inextricably linked like the other great double acts: Fred Astaire and Ginger Rogers, Laurel and Hardy, Rodgers and Hammerstein.

For the twenty-three years that they knew each other, Lennon and McCartney's creative and personal relationship ran the gamut of human emotions, from the kinship of their teenage years and the camaraderie of the Beatlemania era, to an open and bitter feud and, finally, an uneasy truce. John compared their partnership both to a marriage and to a sibling rivalry, and undoubtedly Paul McCartney's influence on his life was comparable only to that of Yoko Ono.

The historic first meeting of Lennon and McCartney took place on Saturday 6 July 1957 at a church fete near John's house in Woolton. A mutual friend, Ivan Vaughan, brought his Liverpool Institute school chum Paul to see his neighbourhood friend John's skiffle group the Quarry Men. The

> *'I had a group. I was the singer and the leader. I met Paul and I made the decision whether to have him in or not – was it better to make the group stronger or to let me be stronger? – and that decision was to let Paul in. Instead of going for an individual thing we went for the strongest format and for equals.'*
>
> JOHN LENNON

two teenagers made a big impression on each other that day. Paul was struck by John's adventurous look, especially his checked shirt, and also by his improvisation of lyrics for the Del-Vikings' 'Come Go With Me'. When they met afterwards in the church hall, the fifteen-year-old McCartney was taken aback by the beery presence of the more mature seventeen-year-old Lennon. Still, he proceeded to dazzle John with his accomplished word-perfect rendition of 'Twenty Flight Rock', an intricate song recently featured by Eddie Cochran in the film *The Girl Can't Help It*.

At this initial meeting the differences in their characters were apparent, but even then they had the potential to be complementary. Where John had begun to experiment by improvising lyrics to a song, Paul had shown the persistence and patience necessary to mimic someone who, in Britain at least, was still relatively obscure (Eddie Cochran's string of UK hits began sixteen months later with 'Summertime Blues').

John recognised that if he asked Paul to join his group, the Quarry Men would gain a talented singer-guitarist, and though this would make them musically more proficient, his own role as leader

Paul McCartney's first image of John Lennon

would be more assailable. Nevertheless, Paul was invited to join up, becoming a member a couple of months later, their passion for rock and roll forming the basis of a friendly long-term alliance.

Having established a solid bond of friendship, the two teenagers began to write music together, initially in an attempt to emulate the style of Buddy Holly. Facing one another with their acoustic guitars, they bounced ideas back and forth, refining their songwriting technique.

Although their songs were credited to Lennon/McCartney, the actual input from one or other would vary. They could both be complete writers and there are songs in their catalogue clearly composed by only one of them. But with a cautious eye to the future, it was decided that to gain credibility with the show business establishment they should always be credited as a songwriting partnership, like Rodgers and Hammerstein, Lerner and Loewe and their favourite pop combination of Goffin and King. 'We wanted to be the Goffin and King of England' John remembered in 1970.

As a rule, Lennon/McCartney songs were sung by their main composer, but the other partner always had an influence which should not be overlooked. 'Norwegian Wood' is usually seen as a pure Lennon song, yet it was Paul's idea for the strange conclusion, in which a flat was burned down, 'So I lit a fire, isn't it good, Norwegian Wood.' Surprisingly, even with the typically Lennonesque 'Lucy In The Sky With Diamonds', a phrase like 'newspaper taxis' came from Paul.

Similarly, McCartney songs like 'Eleanor Rigby' and 'Getting Better' did benefit lyrically from his co-writer's help. The brightness of 'I've got to admit it's getting better' was tinged by the typical cynicism of John's idea that 'it can't get no worse'.

Another benefit of the partnership was that an unfinished piece could be completed with the other's contribution. Again, the optimism in Paul's 'We Can Work It Out' was tempered by John's impatient fifteen bars beginning 'Life is very short and there's no time for fussing and fighting', and with John's 'In My Life', Paul helped with the musical development of the middle-eight over which a baroque piano solo was played. Sometimes two separate songs could be fused together into one, as with 'A Day In The Life', in which Paul's schoolboy memory of 'Woke up, fell out of bed, dragged a comb across my head' was slotted into the contemporary nightmare visions haunting John's song. The urgency to fulfil a deadline would often be the spur to finish songs in this way, and throughout the group's career the two of them remained remarkably prolific.

Another reason for their success as writers was the element of competition between them. As Paul recalls, 'If he had a great idea, I wanted to have a great idea, and I think we always felt we were equal in talent. I don't think I ever looked at John and thought, "Oh, there goes a genius" and I don't think he ever looked at me that way.' While composing best-selling hits, the duo rarely acknowledged how beautiful or stirring these songs were. 'Generally, we just got on with it,' says Paul, 'though there was once, when we were listening through to my "Here, There and Everywhere" when he said, "You know, I think I might like your stuff better than mine". That was the only time he ever said it, and it was quite a lot for someone like John to admit. Then I'd say, "I love 'In My Life', those words are great". We'd compliment each other, but not much, that was for other people to do.'

Certainly, when they wrote apart, the

Top In perfect harmony at a BBC radio recording session, 1963
Bottom Paul McCartney and John Lennon united by a common bond: their passion for rock and roll, and R & B

knowledge that their songs would be played for the other's approval would affect its evolution significantly, and – if only subconsciously – each would try to impress the other or compete for the A-side of the next single. Indeed, artistic rivalry led to some Beatles' singles being promoted as double A-sides. In February 1967, one of the finest pop singles ever released showed just how much Lennon and McCartney could inspire each other's writing in this manner. Both sides of the record dreamily conjured up the writers' Liverpudlian memories. John's 'Strawberry Fields Forever' was a sad, moody piece, full of self-doubt, isolation and longing; Paul's 'Penny Lane' was an optimistic, almost jaunty, trip into nostalgia. Each composer was at the peak of his creativity, yet they were actually writing entirely separately.

John and Paul's close-knit friendship had developed through the shared experience of struggle in Hamburg and Liverpool, and through the united front they presented to the world during Beatlemania. But their fame saw them develop quite distinct interests outside the group. By 1965, John was the author of two idiosyncratic books and was clearly influenced by the example of Bob Dylan's songwriting style. Paul, meanwhile, was keen to develop an interest in the avant-garde scene and to explore the use of classical instruments in his music, such as the string quartet that accompanied him on 'Yesterday'. The Beatles' producer George Martin attributes this interest to Paul's friendship with the family of his girlfriend, Jane, with whom he was living as lodger. 'The Ashers were very upper-middle class musical people, so Paul was subjected to Bach, Handel, Brahms and Beethoven by the very nature of being in that family. For instance, the trumpet in "Penny Lane" came about because he happened to hear a Brandenburg Concerto, noticed a very high piccolo trumpet and said "Can we use that?"'

George Martin was perfectly placed to observe the different characteristics of Lennon and McCartney. 'John didn't give a damn about what anybody thought, Paul did. Paul wanted people to think he was nice, it didn't matter to John. And that came out in their work too, because Paul would tend to write music that was acceptable, John would write music that *he* thought was right, and if people didn't like it, tough on them.'

Consequently, Paul's songs had much more commercial success than his partner's, thereby – through the Lennon/McCartney 50/50 split – earning John a disproportionate amount of royalties. But it would be careless only to think of John as the tough, uncompromising rocker, and Paul as the sensitive balladeer. On the same day that he recorded 'Yesterday', Paul rocked through his Little Richard inspired belter 'I'm Down', while John was equally capable of the two extremes, from the brash cockiness of 'Day Tripper' to the gentleness of 'In My Life'. However, their writing partnership did provide the perfect counterbalance for each other's strengths and weaknesses. Once more, George Martin's comments are illuminating: 'Paul would help John musically because I think that he had a greater understanding of the theory of music and harmony, and he would be able to make something more rounded. John tended to drive the car without a clutch, he'd just go from one gear to another. On the other hand, John was much more of a word merchant. Paul always tended to think of his songs as being music to which he would add lyrics, whereas John tended to think of an idea and a lyric, which had to have a piece of music attached to it. He would have more mastery of imagery in words

Top **Together during one last tour in 1966**
Bottom **Returning from New York,**
where they announced the formation of Apple Corps
in May 1968

and make Paul work harder at his lyrics.'

The release of *Sgt Pepper's Lonely Hearts Club Band* in 1967 marked the virtual end of a close-working writing relationship. John expressed a dislike for the album's 'concept', its segued tracks and playful use of sound effects. 'It was a beautiful idea then, it was cohesive, but it doesn't mean a thing now,' he said in 1969. It had been Paul's desire, encouraged by George Martin, to develop the notion of an LP as more than simply a collection of individual tracks, and this difference of opinion with John was just one of many that occurred in the post-touring era of the Beatles.

It was principally John Lennon and George Harrison who had insisted that Beatles' concerts should be stopped, when the bedlam reached its height on the 1966 North American tour, with its record-burning and fundamentalist outrage over John's 'We're more popular than Jesus' remark. Paul McCartney, Ringo Starr and the Beatles' manager Brian Epstein accepted the decision, but with less enthusiasm. While John detested the by-products of success – the compromises, fanatical adulation, social humiliation and musical frustration – Paul McCartney was more buoyant as the tide of Beatlemania swept him along. 'I still don't think the worship was anything called "pressure",' he says. 'To a large degree, while most of it was going on, we enjoyed it. I've just read about an artist who figures that she'll get ill if she stops working. It was a bit like that, while we were working we had all this stuff in common and most of it was really great, but once we started not to work, once we had time to spend our money, we began to think, "I'm a pretty important dude", and *that* was when the trouble started happening. We had time "to get ill" . . . so we did.'

The unity of the Beatles became more fragile when Brian Epstein died on 27 August 1967, just a year after their last concert. Occurring at a time when John later described his ego as being repressed by heavy use of LSD, Epstein's death caused a power shift within the group. It was Paul McCartney who steered them into *Magical Mystery Tour*, an inventive but flawed film project shown on television at Christmas in 1967. In his angry interview with *Rolling Stone* editor Jann Wenner, John declared: 'Paul made an attempt to carry on as if Brian hadn't died, by saying, "Now, now boys, we're going to make a record". Paul had a tendency to say he'd written his ten songs, let's record now. And I would say "Well, give us a few days, and I'll knock a few off".'

Following the tense, argumentative sessions for the 1968 'White Album', the Beatles were filmed rehearsing and recording the LP that eventually became *Let It Be*. The director Michael Lindsay-Hogg observed them during January 1969, a crucial month for the future of both the Beatles and the Lennon/McCartney partnership. 'It seemed to me that John, who was the general, had been laid low, and Paul, who had been the perfect lieutenant, was forced to take charge . . . he was having to take charge when the general had been hit.' John's bitter accusation that *Let It Be* was 'set up by Paul for Paul', is countered by Lindsay-Hogg's belief that, 'The picture appears very one-sided because one was doing a lot and one was doing nothing. That was when they were breaking up, and Paul didn't want them to break up.' In a crucial scene shot at Apple Studios, the camera captured John impassively smoking and nodding as his partner tried to excite him about further Beatles' projects. Clearly, John did not care anymore.

Lennon eloquently described the situation in a 1976 interview with friend and broadcaster Elliot Mintz: 'I've compared it to a marriage ... it was a long relationship that started many many years before the public knew us, and what happened was that through boredom and through too much of everything – Epstein was dead and people were bothering us with business – the whole pressure finally got to us. Like people do when they're together, we started picking on each other and it became petty. You know, "It's because of you, you got the tambourine wrong, that my whole life is a misery!" Maybe it was the camera of *Let It Be*, the idea that we were going to try and create something phony, that was hard for us. We could see through each other and therefore we felt uncomfortable, because up till then we really believed intensely in what we were doing ... suddenly we didn't believe.'

The root of John's dissatisfaction went back to the end of touring, in 1966, when he began to ponder what life might be like without the Beatles. But it was the arrival of Yoko Ono in May 1968 that caused him to veer away from the group and, most importantly, from his creative ally and rival Paul McCartney. Her presence drove a wedge between John and Paul, and their partnership duly splintered over the next two years. Recalling her impact at that time, Paul says: 'Yoko was exciting his sense of rebellion, and I think that was one of the reasons he found us a bit boring. But I think that was the thing, he got let off the leash and he was ready for some fun. He was ready for a run and anyone that tried to hold him back at that period was just seen as a fool.'

In Yoko Ono, John had found an artistic partner to replace Paul as his chief collaborator, and the free-spirited couple embarked upon a series of projects far removed from the Beatles' music. One was the sound collage album *Two Virgins* which aroused considerable controversy with its cover photographs of John and Yoko naked. When they met EMI Chairman Sir Joseph Lockwood to insist that the sleeve be used, Paul also attended the meeting and attempted to reduce the obvious tensions through his polite diplomacy. A compromise solution was found whereby EMI would press the record, but Apple would have to find another distributor. The Who's label, Track Records, came to the rescue, selling *Two Virgins* in a plain brown paper wrapper. In small print beneath one of the problematic pictures was a quotation from Paul: 'When two great Saints meet it is a humbling experience'.

But Paul's patience was being tried. Continually at John's side, Yoko was present in the recording studio and at Apple business meetings; and Paul, George and Ringo became anxious about whether she might be affecting the future direction of the Beatles. In turn John was frustrated that, particularly during the *Let It Be* sessions, he and George were mere 'sidemen for Paul', so there was obvious disharmony within the group.

An even greater rift opened when Allen Klein – the man appointed by John, George and Ringo to disentangle the chronic state of the group's business affairs – was fiercely rejected by Paul. He favoured his new in-laws, American showbusiness lawyers Lee and John Eastman, but was opposed by the others, most vehemently by John. The charismatic, street-smart Klein had won over the Lennons to such a degree that the more he was resisted, the more fragile became Lennon and McCartney's partnership. It shattered with the Beatles' rancorous split amid lawsuits, bitter recriminations and angry finger-pointing.

In late 1971, some eighteen months after the break-up, John told the BBC that the problems had been exacerbated by lawyers. 'They say "Don't talk to the other party unless there's a lawyer present", and that's when the drift really starts happening because there's no communication. It always gets nasty and you get frustrated and end up saying and doing things you wouldn't really do under normal circumstances.'

Since 1969, through open letters and bitchy interviews, the media had been fed a diet of public squabbling and bitter back-biting between Lennon and McCartney, and the feud also spilled into their music. On Paul's album *Ram*, he tilted at John and Yoko with lines like 'Too many people preaching practices, don't let them tell you what you want to be'.

John's musical retaliation was 'How Do You Sleep', a vicious attack on his former partner, released on the LP *Imagine* in October 1971. With a reference to the ridiculous 'Paul Is Dead' rumours of late 1969, John wrote 'Those freaks was right when they said you was dead.' Comparing a McCartney classic with a recent solo single, he sang, 'The only thing you done was "Yesterday", and since you're gone you're just "Another Day".' The final punch was delivered with the mocking assertion, 'You must have learned something in all those years'.

Such an acidic song did nothing to heal their deep hurting wounds, and John and Paul remained unreconciled for a few more years. However, during John's 'lost weekend' separation from Yoko in 1974, the McCartneys visited the Los Angeles studio where Lennon was producing a Harry Nilsson album. The former partners jammed together – with Paul playing drums – on the old song 'Midnight Special'. John's companion at this time, May Pang, was present at further Lennon-McCartney reunions and recalls, 'Paul would come over and he would just love to sit at a piano and sing. And there were

times, later on, when John said to me, "What do you think, if I started to write with Paul again?"'

John's friend, former Apple promotions man Tony King, also remembers the possibility of a new collaboration between the two. 'He wanted to work with him again, he just couldn't work out the common ground at that time. All that Apple business was still in the way. John loved Paul, no doubt about it. He once said to me, "I'm the only person who's allowed to say nasty things about Paul. I don't like it when other people do." He knew what he didn't like about Paul, but he also knew what he liked about him.' Significantly, when Lennon appeared in concert with Elton John at New York's Madison Square Garden on 28 November 1974, one of the three songs he chose to sing was 'I Saw Her Standing There', written – as he announced – 'by an old estranged fiancé of mine'.

During the years 1975 to 1980, his 'house-husband' period, John concentrated on raising his son Sean, and also learnt how to cook and bake bread. For Paul, the domestic 'ordinariness' of this existence of John's helped in patching up the relationship. 'At least I could relate to that, he'd say "How's the kid?" I'd say "Oh, my little kid's like this". And we could talk babies, cats, and stuff. John was much more accessible and probably more lovable ... he was a darling then, because he was just so generous and warm.'

Yoko Ono, however, questions the depth of the renewed friendship between John and Paul during the latter half of the 1970s: 'If the truth be told, the love was lost both ways, and it was a very healthy situation where they outgrew each other's company. So when John died, before the big reverence was noticed, there were some things that Paul said [from which] I know

Paul and Linda McCartney's album *Ram* was released in
May 1971, with a cover shot of Paul on his Scottish farm.
Five months later, John's album *Imagine* included a
postcard which was a ruthless parody

he was not that enamoured with John. And *now* it might be important for Paul that the world knows John loved him, because it's important that the person who is revered did love him. But if John had died and nobody cared, Paul wouldn't have said that.'

Only John Lennon and Paul McCartney knew the true state of their relationship, but it is hard to doubt the sincerity of Paul's 1982 recording 'Here Today'. Addressed to John it says: 'But as for me, I still remember how it was before. And I am holding back the tears no more, I love you.' Ten years after John's death, Paul feels: 'We are a part of each other's lives, I don't feel we are ever going to be apart. There's something deeper than all the business troubles and through it all, there was always the John that would just pull down his glasses and say, "It's only me, it's only Johnny ... it's a joke really". No matter how bad it got – the fights or the slanging matches – we still kind of liked each other.'

With A Little Help From My Friends

John Lennon's alliance with Paul McCartney was a particularly close and complex partnership. But he also enjoyed a number of other influential relationships with friends, with business managers and with contemporary musicians.

Fellow Beatle George Harrison entered John's life in February 1958, when George was a pupil at the Liverpool Institute school situated next door to John's art college. Just as he had done with Paul McCartney seven months earlier, John evaluated the merits of inviting the budding guitarist to join his skiffle outfit the Quarry Men, while acutely aware that George was virtually two-and-a-half years younger, a yawning gap in teenage terms.

John recalled the circumstances in his December 1970 interview with *Rolling Stone* editor Jann Wenner, exaggerating the age difference to heighten the drama. 'Paul introduced me to George and I listened to him and said, "Play 'Raunchy'" [a Bill Justis instrumental in the charts that month], and I let him in. But George was ten years younger than me, or some shit like that, and I couldn't be bothered with him ... he used to follow me around like a kid, hanging around all the time. It took me years to start considering him as

> '*Paul, George and Ringo –
> that was* then. *And there
> are old school friends,
> people I went to college with,
> but I don't grieve
> ... It's all over.*'
>
> JOHN LENNON

an equal.'

As the years passed, and Beatlemania drew the group closer together, the age difference between John and George diminished in importance, and the pair established a close bond of adult friendship in the latter half of the 1960s. However, George Harrison was certainly aware of the role that he perceived John and Paul wished him to fulfil. As he told BBC Radio 1 DJ Alan Freeman in 1974, 'An attitude came over John and Paul ... you know, "We're the grooves and you two just watch it!". They never said or did anything but ... I always felt a bit like an observer of the Beatles, even though I was one of them, whereas I think that John and Paul were "the stars".'

Following the Beatles' split, indeed to the present day, George has bemoaned how he would have to endure the recording of perhaps a dozen Lennon/McCartney songs for an album before one or two of his own would be considered. It reached the point in 1970, when recording his first solo album, that George had enough unused compositions for a triple-set. John Lennon understood George's frustration, as he told Jann Wenner in 1970, 'He was working with two brilliant songwriters and he learnt a lot from us. I wouldn't have minded being George, the invisible man, and learning what he learnt. Maybe it was hard sometimes for him, because Paul and I are such egomaniacs, but that's the game ...'

A man of considerable wisdom, George offered the BBC the following insight into John Lennon in 1974. 'He's an amazing person. He is brilliant, no question about it. John Lennon is a saint, he's great and I love him. But, at the same time, he's such a bastard! But that's the great thing about him, because he keeps you on your toes. He was always the fighter, the loud-mouth, the shouter and the one with the boot first. And we've all changed a lot. I was the quiet one, on the surface. I don't feel as if I owe John anything, I don't owe Paul a thing, or Ringo anything. I've certainly given them whatever I could and I've taken from them whatever I could.'

George concluded by stating that he would be 'ready to join a band with John Lennon any time. At this point I'm really ready to get down there with him and kick down a few doors, and a few walls and bridges, listen to John's new record *Walls And Bridges*. Fantastic, man, God bless you!'

Sadly, however, despite any reparation in the mid-1970s, George and John were not on the best of terms when John was killed in December 1980. They had not seen each other for some time, and in one of his last interviews John had accused his former Beatle partner of unjustly over-looking his influence and songwriting assistance in the 1960s. Despite this, however, George was gracious enough to inject only the positive aspects of their relationship into a touching tribute song to John, 'All Those Years Ago', issued in May 1981, 'Living with good and bad, I always looked up to you'.

John always enjoyed a great rapport with Ringo Starr, from before the drummer joined the Beatles all the way through to 1980. In the solo years, Lennon was pleased that the least prolific former Beatle had successfully found what he called 'a niche'. Though the much-rumoured Beatles' reunion of the 1970s never occurred, the closest incident took place in March 1973, when both John and George joined Ringo for a recording session. They taped the Lennon song 'I'm The Greatest' for the album *Ringo*. The producer of that Los Angeles session was Richard Perry, and it's a memory he will always treasure. 'When John had come into town and told Ringo that he'd written something for him, Ringo was visibly moved and really couldn't wait for John to come to the studio. John came in and the first thing we did was to play him the tracks that we had done, to which he responded very enthusiastically. In fact, to witness John Lennon's enthusiasm was just another small part of his magic. He always had the tremendous enthusiasm and spirit of a teenager; he held nothing back and if he really loved something his fist went up into the air and he was shout-ing and screaming, giving his approval.

'We were in the middle of constructing some of the chord progressions when someone told me that Mal Evans [formerly one of the Beatles' assistants, loyal to George and Ringo until his death in 1976] was on the phone, on behalf of George. Mal said, "We hear there's a session going on, is it OK if George comes down?" So I said, "Hold on a minute", and as I started to slowly walk from the control room back into the studio I said to myself, "You, Richard Perry, are about to ask John Lennon and Ringo Starr if it's OK if George Harrison comes down to play on the session. Thank you, Lord!" And John's response was, "Hell, tell him to get his ass down here and help me finish this bridge!"'

Hugging Ringo and George at a dinner party
to launch *Sgt Pepper's Lonely Hearts Club Band*
London, May 1967

John with George Harrison and the James Dean-like Stuart
Sutcliffe in Hamburg, late-summer 1960, a day at the fair
preceding another few hours of booze, debauchery and no-
nonsense rock and roll at the Kaiserkeller night-club

Since his relationship with the former Beatles' drummer was less competitive than with either Paul or George, John was often willing to give Ringo any assistance he might require, and helped him with tracks for the albums *Goodnight Vienna* and *Ringo's Rotogravure*. For the latter, in 1976, John even stepped out from his 'house-husband' lifestyle to give Ringo a new composition, 'Cookin' (In The Kitchen Of Love)', and help in recording it. In the autumn of 1980, immediately prior to his death, John was preparing a batch of new songs to give exclusively to Ringo for a 1981 album project. It was typical of Ringo that he should be the only ex-Beatle to comfort Yoko Ono not only by telephone but in person, by making the journey to New York immediately after her husband's murder.

Among the strongest influences in the life of John Lennon was a fellow art college student Stuart Sutcliffe, whom he first met in September 1957 and, for nearly five years, shared the closest of friendships, ending only with Stuart's appallingly premature death at the age of twenty-one. For just over a year, Stuart was bass guitarist in the Beatles, having been encouraged by John to spend some of his money received for some art work on an instrument lacking from the Beatles' line-up.

Sutcliffe played a crucial role in shaping John's teenage aspirations, attitudes and appearance, as fellow art student Bill Harry recalls: I thought that Stuart looked great ... he always used to wear tinted glasses, because one of the influences of the time was Cybulski, an actor who'd appeared in a trilogy of films by Andrzej Wajda, and who was called the Polish James Dean because he had this inarticulate way of being articulate. By putting on the moods and looks, not by speaking, people understood that here was a tormented teenager. And Stuart wore these tinted glasses too, with the hair style and the turned-up collar. I think a lot of John's taste in the Beatles came from the influence of Stuart: in dress, in look, in a certain philosophy.'

On the surface, John and Stuart's friendship seemed to be based on the maxim that 'opposites attract'. Here was the quiet, deep-thinking, passionate painter befriending the loud-mouthed, impetuous, Teddy Boy rocker. Stuart admiring John's rebellious nature while in turn, for John, representing the dedicated intellectual. According to Stuart's sister Pauline, however, this could be an over-simplification of the relationship. 'I'm not so sure now that it was as compart-mentalised as that,' she says. 'I really do feel that they both had features that flowed either way. They were both dedi-cated people, John was as committed and dedicated to being a rocker as Stuart was to being a painter. This was mutual, they had something in common.'

Bill Harry observed John and Stuart together for some time and further recalls that, despite their kinship, Stuart was not exempt from John's cruel humour. 'People could take advantage of a creative intro-vert like Stuart,' asserts Harry. 'You couldn't bully him, or he would clam-up. And John did try to dominate Stu. But I also witnessed that he really got to love him as a friend, and respect his opinion.'

This respect was evidently mutual. In sorting through her late brother's legacy of canvases and papers, Pauline Sutcliffe uncovered an unfinished, unpublished novel, *Spotlight On Johnny*, which could only have been written with John Lennon in mind. 'From reading it, it's quite clear that Stuart understood him,' states Pauline. 'What's disclosed is Stuart's understanding of his [Lennon's] personal pain, and those early severances in his life, his mother's death, and so on. I think some of the closeness was there because they were very intimate about who they were and how they behaved in certain ways. John and Stuart did become the closest of friends.'

Stuart Sutcliffe's influence on John Lennon diminished slightly when, soon after the Beatles' first trip to Hamburg in 1960, Stuart moved there permanently to live with girlfriend Astrid Kirchherr. He died there on 10 April 1962, following a brain haemorrhage. John Lennon learnt of the tragic news the next day, when, ironically, the Beatles arrived back in Germany for another Hamburg club residency. 'The others just turned away,' says Pauline, 'it was John that cried, but I think that he blocked it out after that ... though I also feel that some of the attractiveness of Yoko for John was that she was a woman who embodied some of those radical avant-garde "intellectual" qualities that Stuart had.'

The death of Stuart Sutcliffe dealt another enormous blow to John Lennon in these emotionally formative years. His father had abandoned him, his mother had left him in the care of her sister, and then been killed, and now a friend with whom he had enjoyed a rare degree of closeness, had died aged just twenty-one. The pain was accumulating.

John enjoyed a curious relationship with Brian Epstein, under whose astute managerial guidance the Beatles went from local stardom to worldwide domination. Epstein was a homosexual, and it is believed that his fascination for John Lennon was one of the prime motivations behind his signing the Beatles, especially since – apart from being manager of a record store – he had shown no previous interest in either rock and roll music or the management of artists. Since John Lennon's death, with neither party able to answer the allegations, speculation has mounted that he and Epstein had a brief homosexual relationship during a Spanish holiday they took together in 1963, just three weeks after John's wife Cynthia had given birth to their son, Julian. In Liverpool at least, these rumours were rife at the time, and John did indeed answer back, assaulting a local disc-jockey friend at Paul's 21st birthday party that June after the DJ had passed insinuating remarks about his sexual preferences. 'I must have had a fear that maybe I was a homosexual to attack him like that', John told the BBC in December 1980.

Because of his affection for John, Brian Epstein could be crushed more than most by his barbed remarks. George Martin recalls one particular incident at a 1963 recording session when, while John was attempting to overdub a vocal track, Epstein entered the studio control room. 'He'd obviously had a good dinner,' Martin says. 'He'd had a good bottle of wine and was quite red in the face, and he had his friend in tow. As John finished, Brian smiled at his friend and reached beyond me and pressed the intercommunication button – he'd never done this before, I think he was showing off really – and said something about the way he should sing. And John, who could put down people better than anyone I know – John was the cruellest man alive, in spite of the fact that he was very lovable too – looked up and said, "Brian, you look after the money, we'll look after the music, right?" And Brian went even redder, jumped back as if he'd had an electric shock, and didn't say another word.'

'Brian was a beautiful guy,' John told the BBC in 1971, 'an intuitive, theatrical guy who knew we had something and presented us well. But he had lousy business advice. We were all taken advantage of, Brian included.'

After Epstein's death in August 1967 at the age of just 32, the Beatles remained without a manager until early 1969. It was then that Lennon moved to appoint New Yorker Allen Klein as their business representative. While directing the group's *Let It Be* movie, director Michael Lindsay-Hogg, who had recently worked with the Rolling Stones on their *Rock And Roll Circus* project, overheard a conversation between John Lennon and the other Beatles. 'He was saying, "I met this guy, he's an orphan, he really wants to do good in the world and he knows a lot about the music business. His name is Allen Klein and we ought to meet him." With the Rolling Stones having been represented by Allen Klein for a couple of years, I knew that Mick Jagger and Keith Richards felt that he [Klein] may not have been all that he seemed to be, and that they were not totally happy with him. I went over to Mick and said what I had heard and he said, "My God, that's terrible . . .", and I remember walking around with him to Savile Row. His aim was to speak to John and say that perhaps this was not such a good idea.'

'I told them they were ridiculous to think about signing with him because we were actually suing Allen Klein at the time,' states Jagger. 'I told them that we regretted it [signing with Klein]. John certainly was the prime mover, probably because he didn't really want to think about business. He always thought of himself as the "romantic artist" who didn't want to think about it. But if you don't you end up not being a "romantic artist" because you have to get out of all these entanglements and spend all your time on them.'

Mick Jagger's advice fell on deaf ears, especially those of John Lennon, who had been struck by the affable charm of the charismatic and undeniably successful Allen Klein. Rarely was there ever a more loyal person than John Lennon, and he doggedly supported Klein's cause through the battle with Paul McCartney (who resisted Klein's appointment), through the court case Paul brought to dissolve the Beatles' legal partnership, and through to 1973, when Klein's contract was not renewed by Apple Corps. Their association ended there, apart from a lawsuit that brought the two sides into open conflict, not settled for a further four years. John's 1974 song 'Steel And Glass' publicised the disharmony, with its stinging anti-Klein sentiments, very reminiscent in terms of musical style and degree of viciousness to his anti-McCartney track 'How Do You Sleep'.

In 1970, however, there was no sign of the future disenchantment when, referring to his first proper meeting with Klein at the end of January 1969, John told *Rolling Stone*: 'He not only knew my work and the lyrics that I'd written from way back, he knew what I was saying. He's an intelligent guy who told me what was happening with the Beatles and my relationship with Paul, George and Ringo. He knew every damn thing about us. Anybody that knew me that well without ever meeting me had to be a guy that I could allow to look after me. Allen is a human being, the same as Brian was a human being. It was the same thing as with Brian in the early days, it was assessment. I make a lot of mistakes, character-wise, but now and then I make a good one. And Allen's one, Yoko's another, and Brian was one. I'm closer to him [Klein] than anybody, outside of Yoko.'

'Steel And Glass' was recorded and released in 1974, during John's 'lost weekend'. One often overlooked facet of this period is that John was more productive then than at any other time since the break-up of the Beatles in 1970. Apart

Apart from their albums and acorn events, bed-ins and
bagism, John and Yoko made and produced a number of
avant-garde films. Here they oversee the editing of their
latest effort *Rape*, in early 1969

from recording two albums, he teamed up with a number of fellow musicians for studio recordings, a live concert appearance and jam sessions. One such Los Angeles studio jam, recording the soul number 'Too Many Cooks', was the subject of considerable Lennon production effort and featured Mick Jagger, Stevie Wonder and a host of hot session players. Though at that time it could never have been issued because each musician was contracted to a different record company, muses Mick Jagger today, 'I don't even know what happened to the tape . . .'

John's most regular partner in Los Angeles between late 1973 and mid-1974 was Harry Nilsson, the successful singer and writer who had released a string of albums over the previous six years and scored an international hit with 'Without You' in 1972. Nilsson recalls stumbling upon John and his *Rock 'n' Roll* album producer Phil Spector at the A&M Studios one night. 'It was a time when I was really depressed and down and looking for anyone to have a drink or be with. I went to every bar in town, called all my friends, there was no one. So then I started studio hopping and the last stop on the list was A&M. I opened the door and there was every friend I ever had in my whole life. It happened to be at a time when they were in a war and I became a maypole they could both dance around for that moment.

'One thing led to another and then Phil said that he couldn't work with John anymore because John was getting too loaded – it was probably his frustration with Phil more than anything – and John said, "I'm gonna produce Harry Nilsson!" I never questioned it but a few days later he called and said, "Well, what songs are we gonna do?" '

The resulting album, *Pussy Cats*, sums up the chaotic first half of the 'lost weekend'. Instead of the mellifluous vocal style that was his trademark, Nilsson croaked his way through the sessions, opting to keep a secret the fact that he was, as John later noted, 'bleeding in the throat', a condition exacerbated by the considerable quantities of liquor consumed by the singer and most of the musicians at the recording sessions.

Typically, it was John who pulled back from the brink, though he later admitted to there having been '*some* moments' at the Santa Monica beachside house he shared with Harry, Keith Moon and Ringo Starr. 'Suddenly I was the straight one in the middle of all these mad, mad people,' John told the BBC's Bob Harris in 1975. 'I was suddenly not one of them and I pulled myself back and finished off the album as best I could.' To do this, John quit Los Angeles and flew back to New York with May Pang to complete the LP, all the time trying to keep Harry at arm's length. It was in New York, however, that Lennon and Nilsson wrote a song together, 'Old Dirt Road', issued on *Walls And Bridges*.

Other important collaborations followed. Lennon was invited to contribute to David Bowie's version of the Beatles' track 'Across The Universe' and, while at the session, he helped compose 'Fame' with Bowie and his guitarist Carlos Alomar. The song became Bowie's first US number one single.

'Fame' had its origins in 'Shame, Shame, Shame', a contemporary disco hit by Shirley and Company, a copy of which was given to Lennon by friend and former Apple promotions executive Tony King, now working for Elton John. King was also instrumental in bringing together his old and new employers for a productive period that saw them collaborate on each other's records and prompted Lennon to do something he'd not done in more than

John with Harry Nilsson, in a more sober moment in New York, during the annual March Of Dimes ceremonies, May 1974. With them is famous US radio DJ 'Cousin Brucie'

two years, perform in concert. Recalled John in his 6 December 1980 BBC interview: 'He did the harmony and played beautiful piano on "Whatever Gets You Thru The Night" and he was telling me he was going to do this Madison Square Garden concert and jokingly he said, "Will you do it with me if the record is a number one?". I did not expect it to get to number one at all, I didn't think it had a chance in hell, so I said, "Sure I will, sure I will ...".' It was a reasonable wager to make, Lennon had yet to score a post-Beatles number one in the USA, and even 'Imagine' had only reached number three. But make the top it did. 'He came back and said "It's time to pay your dues ..."'

'John had the runs all that day, he was so nervous,' remembers Tony King. 'Yoko had called and asked me to arrange a seat for her, and I got one where John wouldn't be able to see her. Before the show John said to me, "Thank God Yoko's not here, I couldn't do it if I knew she was out there". I think that night is still one of the most exciting moments I've ever seen, because John'd been away for so long and he'd just had a number one record, and when Elton said "A special guest ..." the place went *mad*. The whole of Madison Square Garden shook.'

Though they met backstage after the triumphant concert, it was another two months before John finally reunited with Yoko back at the Dakota, soon conceiving Sean, their only child together. In their great fondness for Elton, they invited him to become the baby's godfather, a position he was honoured to accept. With the dawn of the 'house-husband' years, John's artistic collaborations ceased and he never again had the opportunity to pursue this interesting strand of his life and career.

John and Yoko pictured together at the Grammy Awards on 1 March 1975, their first public appearance since reuniting only days earlier. With them is David Bowie, whom Lennon had just helped to record two tracks, including the future number one single 'Fame'

John's friendship with Elton John and their mutual admiration resulted in Lennon's last ever concert appearance, as special guest at Elton's Thanksgiving Night concert in New York, 28 November 1974

Give Peace A Chance

One of the most evocative images of the 1960s is that of John Lennon and Yoko Ono in bed, straggly hair cascading over their white bed-clothes, urging the world to 'give peace a chance'. The world's reaction was to think that the chief Beatle, who had always been slightly odd, had finally flipped.

Even those who claimed to understand Lennon – few in number at this time, when he seemed to be acting so strangely – concluded that here was another Lennon fad, soon to be discarded after the novelty had worn off. But such people were quite wrong. John Lennon advocated peace for the rest of his life, whether loudly or quietly. It was a subject that he thought through carefully, not one seized upon one rainy afternoon.

John and his fellow Beatles all developed anti-war sympathies soon after becoming famous, although the vehicles through which pop stars were allowed to communicate in those days, typically teen magazines and radio or TV shows all steeped in the variety tradition, afforded them no real outlet by which to express them. The only opportunities for the Beatles to talk seriously were press conferences, but manager Brian Epstein

> *'The message is peace! You can protest about violence in many ways, and this is one ...'*
>
> JOHN LENNON

forbade them to speak publicly on such delicate issues, fearing that it would damage their popularity.

By 1966 though, with American involvement in the Vietnam War escalating, they could no longer hold back. During US press conferences on their final ever concert tour, the Beatles summoned up courage and spoke out. But instead of a backlash there came, surprisingly, nothing; their comments were drowned out by the furore over John's so called 'anti-Jesus' statement and by a still overpowering Beatlemania. However, in June 1967, the Beatles recorded John's composition 'All You Need Is Love'. Jon Wiener, professor of history at the University of California and author of *Come Together: John Lennon In His Time*, the definitive study of Lennon's political years recalls, 'The song was coming out of every window in every college dormitory in the United States that summer. And this was implicitly, I think, very much a criticism of the war-makers in the US, [the Beatles were saying] "you don't need war, all you need is love".' This time they had succeeded in getting their message across, and in a way which instantly grabbed the attention of people all over the world.

But it was in 1968 that John Lennon's

Not so much naive as just plain optimistic,
the Beatles nail their colours to the placards the day before
400 million TV viewers around the world see them record
'All You Need Is Love', 24 June 1967

anti-war position, fermented over several years, finally took a tangible shape and direction, boosted to an incalculable degree by the dawning of his relationship with Yoko Ono. Yoko shared similar views, and with her background in avant-garde art knew exactly how she and John could propagate such a stance through 'events'. John's name alone would attract all the publicity that they could hope to handle and talking in a BBC television interview soon after he had met Yoko he made one of his first bold statements on the subject. He said: 'I think our society is run by insane people for insane objectives ... we're being run by maniacs for maniacal ends. If anybody can put on paper what our government and the American government, the Russians, the Chinese, what they are actually trying to do, I'd be very pleased.' While appreciating that 'half the people watching this are going to be thinking, "What's he saying?"', Lennon concluded the interview by addressing the viewing audience directly, telling them, 'You are being run by people who are insane and you don't know!'

The violence that erupted in 1968 was in remarkable contrast to the previous year and its 'summer of love'. Observing riots on the streets and fists in the air, John put his thoughts on the matter into song, writing 'Revolution' as a direct response to the turbulent events. As Jon Wiener remembers, 'In 1968 we had students nearly overthrowing the government in Paris, we had building seizures on college campuses across the United States ... it was a revolutionary year, but there was a lot of debate and uncertainty about what kind of revolution ought to come into existence. And Lennon's first view was that it ought to be a revolution of *personal* liberation rather than political liberation. Addressing himself directly to

the kids marching in the streets he sang, "You say you want a revolution? You'd better free your minds instead." He was engaging in a debate with political militants, I was one of them and we were very unhappy with his statement. Lennon was somebody we admired and respected and we wanted to argue with him about this.'

John Lennon discussed the summer riots of 1968 from the vantage point of 1969: 'The end product of the Grosvenor Square marches [site of the US Embassy in London] was just newspaper stories about riots and fighting. We did the 'bed event' in Amsterdam and the 'bag peace' in Vienna just to give people an idea that there are many ways of protest and this is one of them, and anybody can grow their hair for peace or give up a week of their holiday for peace or sit in a bag for peace. Protest for peace in any way, but *peacefully.*'

The 'events' in Amsterdam and Vienna were John and Yoko's first major steps in their long-running peace campaign. Such antics were inspired by Yoko's unconventional 'Happenings' in her avant-garde work. It all boiled down to humour, a vital new stratagem in the peace protest armoury. 'That's part of our policy, not to be taken seriously,' affirmed John, 'because our opposition, whoever they may be in all their manifest forms, don't know how to handle humour, and we're humorists. We're willing to be the world's clowns. Laurel and Hardy, that's John and Yoko, and we stand a better chance under that guise because all the serious people like Martin Luther King and Kennedy and Gandhi got shot.'

John himself was not without his violent side, and in Liverpool days had been no stranger to the use of fists. Even as late as June 1963, when the wilder side of his personality was being repressed by Brian Epstein and by the onset of fame,

'After answering all these questions
many, many, many, many, many, many,
many times . . .'

'. . . it got down to, all we were saying was "give peace a
chance!"' John Lennon performing and recording, from
his and Yoko's hotel bed in Montreal, what would swiftly
become the youth's international anthem

Lennon's first major coverage in a national British newspaper occurred, not through pop chart exploits, but over his assault of a former disc-jockey friend at Paul McCartney's 21st birthday party. (Such behaviour would resurface years later too, during the Los Angeles section of the long 'lost weekend' period.) So it was with personal experience that John told an interviewer in 1969, 'I'm as violent as the next man, but I prefer myself when I'm non-violent. I prefer my friends when they're non-violent. If we have to have violence, let's channel it. I don't want to be involved in violence, I prefer to live in peace.'

Recalled John in his December 1980 interview with the BBC's Andy Peebles, 'The point of the bed-in, in a nutshell, was a commercial for peace as opposed to a commercial for war, which was on the news everyday in those days. Everyday there was dismembered bodies, napalm, and we thought, "Why don't they have something nice in the papers?"' The Lennon's first bed-in took place in the Amsterdam Hilton at the end of March 1969, a few days after their wedding on the rock of Gibraltar. Then, two months later, they held a second, similar event. 'We tried to do it in New York,' said John in 1980, 'but the American government wouldn't let us in. They didn't want any peaceniks, so we ended up doing it in Montreal and broadcasting back across the border.'

The two bed-ins for peace shared a simple concept: John and Yoko sat in bed for a week, opened their bedroom door to every conceivable media person, and talked and talked and talked, and then talked some more. Because of his fame and, initially, the intrigue, some thought the Lennons would be publicly making love ('It'd be a very good idea for peace,' John noted at the time, adding, 'but I think I'd probably be the producer of that event ...'), John and Yoko were besieged by journalists, writers, radio and television broadcasters, every day, from morning to night. Patiently, with each interviewer, John and Yoko would plead and reason for peace, putting up with the ridicule and the snide insults that they inevitably attracted.

Lennon remembered: 'After answering all these questions many, many, many, many, many, many, many times, it got down to all we were saying was "give peace a chance". Not that we have any formula, or that communism or socialism will answer it, or any "ism". We didn't have a format, we couldn't give you a plan. But just consider the idea of not having this war, just *consider* it'. Typically, Lennon used his musical intuition and perceptiveness to popularise this message in an effective anthem-like song. 'Give Peace A Chance', his first single outside of the Beatles, was recorded in Room 1742 of the Queen Elizabeth Hotel, Montreal, at the climax of his and Yoko's second bed-in.

'Every political movement needs good songs,' considers Jon Wiener, 'and one of the things that Lennon was able to do was contribute a great song. Within a few months it spread throughout the entire anti-war movement. There were tens of thousands of people singing it, first at protests in New York City and finally in Washington DC.' [On Moratorium Day, 15 November 1969, when 250 000 citizens marched on the Capitol demanding an end to US participation in Vietnam; at a time when its military presence was at a peak of 543 400 personnel.] 'It was a rare and very wonderful event that a new protest song would be written,' notes Wiener, 'and once they had the media's attention they could deliver their peace message in a way that would reach more people. It earned John and Yoko a lot of ridicule from the conservative media but they were amazingly good-natured about that, they were willing to put up with it to get their message across.'

The message certainly did come across. For every patronising jibe made by journalists like Gloria Emerson (captured on film and included in the 1988 *Imagine: John Lennon* documentary movie), 'Oh, my dear boy, you're living in a nether, nether land ... you don't think you've saved a single life?', and for every TV comedian cracking jokes at John and Yoko's expense, the 'advert' hit a wide audience. The Lennons, in turn, were granted an audience with a world leader, the new Canadian prime minister Pierre Trudeau. 'We talked about everything on earth,' John excitedly told a BBC reporter a few weeks later. 'It's like he's running a big business and he can't really know what the doormen and the caretakers are doing, but he cares about them, and he was asking us, as a shop-steward of youth maybe, "What's going on out there?"'

As the 1970s dawned, John, reflecting on the importance of the ten years just ended, said: 'The sixties was a great decade. The great gatherings of youth in America and the Isle of Wight, they might have just been pop concerts to some people, but they were a lot more than that. They were the youth getting together and forming a new church, saying we believe in hope and truth and here we are, 200 000 of us, all together in peace.' John declared 1970 to be 'Year One', a new start.

John and Yoko's high profile as protagonists for the peace movement made them inevitable targets for publicity seekers. The Lennons duly supported the demand for a public enquiry into the allegedly wrongful hanging of the 'A6 murderer' James Hanratty; they associated with the British black-power leader Michael X, later to be executed himself for murder; they marched for the IRA and against the obscenity trial of the British 'underground' paper *Oz*. Lennon staunchly defended these actions, denying any suggestion of having a butterfly-like nature. 'Look, I'm often accused of being a dilettante, and jumping from conkers to marbles, but to me it's all the same,' he stressed. 'If I'm talking about Hanratty or I'm talking about Northern Ireland or Black Power or Red Indians, it's the same to me.'

The essential difference between the 1960s and previous decades of change had been the carefully considered, radical concept that before planning any transformation of society one must first transform oneself. 'It was a dilemma that John Lennon strove to overcome,' believes Jon Wiener. 'I don't think that he solved the problem, but I don't think anybody else has done a very good job of solving it either. To me, his most impressive effort is the *Plastic Ono Band* album, where he brings together some of the most truthful and stark statements about his own personal life that any pop artist has ever made, with attention to the larger issues.' One such song was 'Working Class Hero', in which Lennon stood up and spoke for the working-class masses:

Keep you doped with religion and sex and TV,
And you think you're so clever and classless and free,
But you're still fucking peasants as far as I can see.

Other songs followed, each centred around Lennon's core dedication to peace, even if the approach was varied. The 1971 single 'Power To The People' – written 'as a guilt song' following a visit by Tariq Ali, editor of 'underground' paper *Red Mole* – opened to the sound of marching feet; still for peace, but now out on the streets, demanding action.

Released eight months later, the song 'Imagine' took an altogether different approach, its towering but gentle wisdom shading any suggestion of naivety. By the time it was issued, on the album of the same name, John and Yoko had left England and moved to the United States, setting up first in an hotel and then, characteristic of this period, moving into the type of apartment in Greenwich Village that any artist, beatnik or poet might rent. Here was one of the former Beatles, living in and walking around the bohemian area of New York City, only five years after the group had quit touring amid the mayhem of Beatlemania. For John and Yoko the abandonment of their mansion back in England and the adoption of Greenwich Village life was essential because they wanted to be among 'the people'.

Soon after their arrival in New York, the Lennons linked up with noted radicals Jerry Rubin and Abbie Hoffman. They were two of the celebrated Chicago Seven conspirators, who had been tried for planning a riot during the 1968 Democratic National Convention in Chicago. They had been found not guilty but were sentenced instead for crossing state lines with intent to incite violence; a charge greeted with scorn by many. As Yoko recalls, she and John had followed the trial while they were still living in England. 'We felt they were pretty interesting people,' she says. 'So when we came here [to New York] somehow they got in touch with us, or we got in touch with them . . .'

'Jerry and Abbie were two very important and creative people who were also a lot of fun,' notes Jon Wiener. 'These were the kind of people who were the most interested in the same kind of creative and novel tactics, the kind of media politics that John and Yoko were experimenting with. So it's not at all surprising that John and Yoko would want to get together with them. Rubin worked hard to organise them into his projects.'

John and Yoko quickly became besotted by New York and in particular Greenwich Village life, walking around Washington Square Park, meeting with radical street musician David Peel, and joining forces with him for an Apple album *The Pope Smokes Dope*, and with political bar band Elephant's Memory for a number of other musical projects. And all this time, they were being drawn closer and closer into the Rubin/Hoffman world of counter-culture politics. On 11 December 1971 the Lennons were headline act at a benefit concert in Ann Arbor, Michigan, a rally for the release of John Sinclair, the former political organiser of the White Panther party. He was serving a ten-year prison sentence for selling two marijuana joints to an undercover agent, yet another example of the Establishment's determined stance against radicals. 'They gave him ten for two, what else can the bastards do?' sang John Lennon in a song he wrote especially for the occasion.

Forty-eight hours after the show, Sinclair was suddenly released. John, Yoko, Rubin, Hoffman, Peel, indeed the entire New Left movement, were cock-a-hoop with joy, and formulated plans for a fully-fledged US concert tour, in which the Lennons would attract packed audiences, and the counter-culture message would be disseminated in speech and in song. The tour was planned to coincide with the 1972 party conventions in San Diego and Miami.

First, though, there would be an album, *Some Time In New York City*, recorded in March 1972. The record crystallised John and Yoko's 'newspaper headline' approach to music, writing songs that captured the flavour not only of the year or month but of the week or the very day,

John and Yoko performing 'Instant Karma!' on the BBC-TV show *Top Of The Pops*, 12 February 1970. Since its lyric was less direct than previous Plastic Ono Band singles, John and Yoko ensured that their continuing commitment to peace remained abundantly clear

Backstage at the Lennons' One To One charity concert in New York, 30 August 1972. Either side of session drummer Jim Keltner (centre) are the mean-looking members of Elephant's Memory, the local band which had backed John and Yoko on their heavily political album *Some Time In New York City*. Sprawled on the floor is the enigmatic Phil Spector, record producer extraordinaire

addressing what for them were vital counter-culture and social issues of the moment. The entire album was in this vein: there was 'Angela', a song for jailed black radical Angela Davis; 'The Luck Of The Irish' and 'Sunday Bloody Sunday' were about the troubles in Northern Ireland, and vicious in their anti-British slant. There was 'John Sinclair', first sung at the Michigan rally; there was 'New York City', an updated version of 'The Ballad Of John And Yoko', in which Lennon explained the appeal of the city and named Rubin, Peel and Elephant's Memory along the way. There was 'Attica State', about the jail riots the previous September in which thirty-two prisoners and ten guards had been killed; and there was the hard-hitting feminist statement, 'Woman Is The Nigger Of The World'. It was a brave album for Lennon to make, but one slaughtered by the critics and which sold very poorly by his standards. Bereft of most of its meaning when heard outside of the USA, it also had no chance of remaining relevant as time went by, and dated very quickly.

Around the time of the album's release, John and Yoko pulled the plug on the proposed concert tour. 'John had his own life and ideas,' explains Yoko. 'Jerry and Abbie felt the same kind of feeling that we initially felt, like we were "brothers, baby", but then they suddenly realised that they cannot control us ... We moved away because we realised that we might have a different opinion about certain things.'

There were other reasons too. John's pronouncements about Vietnam and his involvement with the New Left had aroused the interest of President Nixon's administration. Under instruction from the White House, the FBI instigated a policing action against Lennon, while the Immigration and Naturalization Service simultaneously sought to deport him, revoking his visa because of his 1968 London conviction for possession of cannabis. So began a three-year battle in which Lennon fought to remain in the USA. Observes Jon Wiener, 'Lennon's lawyers told him that basically he had no case at all and that if he did anything more along the lines of this anti-war rock and roll campaign he would almost certainly be immediately deported, but if he cooled it, through various legal manoeuvres, he might be able to stay. From then on, Lennon was in court, trying not to get kicked out.'

Though devious and undemocratic, the FBI campaign did, in part, succeed in its aim: John Lennon was effectively muzzled. He loved the USA, particularly New York, and, besides, he and Yoko had moved there for several reasons, one of which was to attempt to retrieve Kyoko, Yoko's daughter from a previous marriage, her ex-husband having absconded with the infant despite a court order assigning her to Yoko's care. Leaving the States would effectively have meant abandoning the search for Kyoko.

Though he was politically silenced, Lennon did speak about the FBI harassment. On *The Dick Cavett Show* he informed a US television audience that he was being followed by the FBI, and that his telephone was being tapped: 'They wanted me to know, to scare me, and I was scared, paranoid!' Lennon told the BBC's Bob Harris in 1975. 'At that time it was pre-Watergate, so you can imagine John Lennon saying that his phone is tapped and there's men following in a car ... But I went on TV and said this was happening to me and it stopped the next day. People thought I was crazy, I mean they do anyway, but more so, you know, "Lennon, oh you big-headed maniac, who's going to follow you around?"'

'If the man wants to shove us out, we're gonna jump and shout, "The Statue of Liberty said 'Come!' " '. Lennon chose an apt backdrop for this 1974 photo session, at a time when he was still appealing against his deportation order

But the FBI continued to harass Lennon for some time. In the early 1980s, when Professor Jon Wiener successfully sued the FBI and the Immigration and Naturalization Service under the Freedom Of Information Act, he received a remarkable stack of papers twenty-six pounds in weight; still more remain classified to this day 'withheld in the interest of the national defense or foreign policy'. It was, clearly, a major offensive operation against a former member of the Beatles, the most celebrated act in popular music history, ecstatically welcomed to the USA on several occasions just a few short years previously.

'It took the resignation of Richard Nixon to lay the groundwork for John to stay [in the United States],' says Wiener. 'Although Lennon was not officially one of the targets exposed in the Watergate case, it's clear that this was a kind of rock and roll Watergate. As soon as Nixon was out, Lennon proceeded pretty quickly to get his immigration case thrown out of court, and eventually the courts agreed that he had been the victim of political persecution.' This was October 1975, and his prized Green Card finally came through in July 1976.

Lennon spent the next four years keeping away from all forms of public life, most especially politics. But in researching his account of John's political career, Jon Wiener discovered that Lennon had planned a return to some form of activism in 1980. 'A cousin of Yoko's was involved in political work with Asian-Americans in Los Angeles,' he reports. 'They were going on strike and appealed to John and Yoko for help. John agreed, drafted a political statement, made plans to join their picket line and actually bought airplane tickets. He was planning to march with his five-year-old son Sean on his shoulders and was shot just a couple of days before he was going to leave.'

Lennon's senseless murder was tragic in so many ways, but one unexpected aspect was highlighted in the latter months of 1989, when the political map of Eastern Europe underwent dramatic, sudden, quite unforeseeable change, brought about by the power of the people. As bulldozers bit chunks out of the Berlin Wall, as repressed peoples crossed hitherto restricted national borders, they did so singing John Lennon songs, 'All You Need Is Love' and 'Give Peace A Chance'. Here was the end result of John's forceful campaigning for peace – virtually as he predicted – and he was not alive to share in the joy.

So uncannily true of 1989, John Lennon said this in 1969: 'There's an ancient Chinese method of fighting war, they say that when you're in the castle, the castle always falls from within. The attacks from outside never happen, but from within the situation is crumbling. These left-wing people talk about giving power to the people. That's nonsense! The people *have* the power, all we're trying to do is make people aware ... And the violent way of revolution doesn't justify the end, there's no peaceful country on earth that had a violent revolution. All we're trying to do is to expose politicians and expose the people themselves who are being hypocritical and sitting back and saying "We can't do anything about it, it's up to somebody else; give us the answer, John". People have to *organise*. It takes time, but it's faster than we think.'

Woman

The 1980 song 'Woman' was one of John Lennon's final statements both about feminism and his love for Yoko Ono, and was one of many songs that gave clues to his treatment of women throughout his life. On the 1964 Beatles album *A Hard Day's Night* there was evidence of both a possessive bravado in 'You Can't Do That', 'If I catch you talking to that boy again, I'm gonna let you down, and leave you flat', and a vulnerable tenderness in 'If I Fell', 'If I love you too, Oh please don't hurt my pride like her'. His behaviour with women echoed these contrasting emotions, and in his relationships gentleness was usually discovered beneath a façade of toughness.

During his life Lennon made the difficult transition from being an instinctive male chauvinist to an ardent feminist, eager to play a part in promoting sexual equality. In fact, during childhood, the experience of his own family's background had initiated a subconscious form of feminist education, being brought up by his Aunt Mimi, one of five sisters on the maternal side of his family. As John's stepsister Julia Baird remembers, 'They were all extremely strong ladies. The men in their lives – my father and our uncles –

> *'It suddenly hit me about what women represent to us, not as the sex object or the mother, but just their contribution. [On "Woman"] you hear me muttering "the other half of the sky", which is Chairman Mao's famous statement. It is the other half ... without each other there ain't nothin'!'*
>
> JOHN LENNON

were very much part of the wallpaper.'

John's mother Julia paid no heed to any moral indignation aroused in 1940s Britain by bearing two daughters by John Dykins while still married to Freddy Lennon. John knew her best during his teenage years, adoring her fun-loving pranks and free-and-easy approach to life. Her sudden death in July 1958 scarred the seventeen-year-old Lennon emotionally, and his immediate defence was to hide his feelings away from the world and from himself.

Around the time of the tragedy, he began a relationship at art college with Cynthia Powell which was to span more than ten years, right through the period of Beatlemania. Her life with John Lennon was always destined to be unusual, as another former student, Bill Harry, recalls, 'Cynthia used to come to the early gigs at places like the Jacaranda [a Liverpool coffee bar]. There was no equipment so she would sit there holding a broom handle with the microphone tied to the end.' In keeping with the widespread chauvinism of the time, John expected Cynthia to be subservient to his whims. Even his absolute adoration of movie actress Brigitte Bardot was imposed on Cynthia. As Bill

Harry remembers, 'He got her in the Bardot style, so her hair went fairer, she had the pony-tail and she dressed like her.'

Despite this apparent dominance, there can be no doubt that John and Cynthia did enjoy a close and reciprocal loving relationship. Letters from Hamburg in the early sixties, and dispatches from Beatles' tours, display not only the depth of his love for Cynthia but how candid he could be with her. 'He did have this exterior of being the hard-knock, but he wasn't at all,' Cynthia told the BBC in 1984. 'He was a loving and caring man, he was vulnerable and, above all else, honest to his own pain. I feel that I had the best years with John ... it sounds a very strange thing to say ... but I feel he was at his most content from 1960 to 1965.'

When Cynthia accidentally fell pregnant in July 1962, John did what propriety demanded and they were married within weeks on 23 August. On their wedding night, John played a concert with the Beatles in Chester; it turned out to be an omen of the frequent future separations they would have to endure. Julian, their only child together, was born the following April and Cynthia immediately strove to create a scene of domestic normality, at least as much as Beatlemania would allow, for John to retreat into. 'I was a homemaker and a mother, that was what presented itself to me at the time,' she says, 'I wouldn't have changed a thing.'

In July 1964, the Lennons moved to a mock-Tudor mansion, Kenwood, in Weybridge, in the 'stockbroker belt' outside London. But during the following years' breaks from touring, filming and recording, John grew dissatisfied with his cushioned and rather isolated home life. Imprisoned by his colossal fame and marked by momentous experiences that Cynthia could not possibly share, he began to drift away from his wife.

In the 1965 song 'Girl', John expressed a fascination with the idea of a partner who would be more challenging than a compliant homemaker, 'She's the kind of girl you want so much it makes you sorry, still you don't regret a single day'. In 1980, he told *Playboy* magazine's David Sheff he had written about a '*dream* girl – the one that hadn't come yet – that was Yoko.'

Yoko Ono entered John's life on 9 November 1966 when he visited a preview of her exhibition *Unfinished Paintings and Objects* at the Indica Gallery in London. He was beguiled by the bizarre pieces on display: one was an apple on a stand priced at £200, another, a stepladder up to a magnifying glass dangling from the ceiling, which when peered through, revealed in minuscule lettering the word *Yes*. When John met the artist, he was intrigued by her off-beat thoughts and she, though unimpressed by his celebrity, warmed to his humour. However, it would be a further eighteen months before they both left their spouses to hurtle headlong into an all-consuming relationship.

Yoko remembers that John 'was in his low period and that stirred my sympathy or emotions. Because I am that kind of strong woman, if a guy is very strong I don't think I would feel too attracted. [John] was suffering and obviously going through something and that made me have a strong feeling for him.' Seven and a half years older than John, Yoko was a free-thinking artist, and although married twice, she had never been a traditional homemaker or mother. John was amazed to discover a woman with whom he could communicate on a level that he thought only possible with a male friend. 'She's me in drag!' he told the BBC in 1969.

Having fallen in love with a Beatle, Yoko quickly discovered the baggage that came with it. Throughout the years of Beatlemania, there had been a remarkable

Cynthia accompanies John to the Foyles Literary Luncheon held in his honour at the Dorchester Hotel, London on 23 April 1964

THE TIMES BUSINESS NEWS

bond of camaraderie between the group, who had a capacity to join forces, close ranks and exclude outsiders. As a result of Yoko's constant presence in the studio, John perceived a chauvinism in his fellow Beatles, who, in his eyes, felt resentment because a *woman* had infiltrated their closely guarded domain. Looking back with the BBC's Andy Peebles in 1980, John explained, 'There'd been four guys very close together and the women never came to the sessions, only for openings when they did their hair. And suddenly Yoko and I were together all the time … in the corner, mumbling and giggling together and then we'd look around and see that we weren't being approved of.'

John had found the antithesis of his first wife in Yoko, a woman who would challenge him, bring out his suppressed interests and encourage his free spirit. No longer pampered by cosy domesticity, he was catapulted into a new life of 'events' for peace, collaboration on records of 'Unfinished Music' and avant-garde films like *Two Virgins*, *Erection* and *Fly*. Michael Lindsay-Hogg remembers a meeting at Apple prior to his direction of the film *Let It Be*, when John played a tape to the other Beatles. 'Whether it was or it wasn't, you assumed from the noises on the tape that it was John and Yoko making love. You didn't know what to say, in the sense, what could you say? Either, "That's nice," or "That sounds very enjoyable for you both". But it was a curious intimacy which John and Yoko wanted to share and no one knew what to make of it. They wanted to branch out and offer up some kind of candour to the world.'

The Beatles might have been shocked by John and Yoko's weird noises, and the world contemptuous of their eccentric bed and bag events for peace, but the Lennons appeared not to care. However, the intensity of their relationship and the bewildering range of their activities had begun to take their toll. 'At the time when people in the world were probably thinking, "Oh they must be lovey-dovey", that's exactly when we were arguing like crazy,' says Yoko. 'It's really to do with having to come together from very different backgrounds, and a lot had to do with jealousy. We had our pasts, and Kyoko [Yoko's daughter born in 1963] was my tie, and that reminded us of Kyoko's father and, of course, being an artist I was working with a lot of people …'

After one particularly jealous outburst from John had temporarily sullied their relationship, he wrote the lyric to one of his finest songs. He turned a whimsical unfinished song about the Beatles' 1968 trip to India, called 'Child Of Nature', into 'Jealous Guy' released on the *Imagine* album in 1971, 'I was dreaming of the past, And my heart was beating fast. I was shivering inside …'. This possessiveness remained a consistent characteristic of his life, and was also revealed in later songs like 'I'm Losing You' and 'Scared', in which he screams, 'Hatred and jealousy, going to be the death of me, I guess I knew it right from the start'.

John may have also understood that, as an artist recognised in her own field, Yoko would find the massive interest in her husband's work somewhat galling. Through his urging, a series of singles and albums by Yoko – often with star rock musicians jamming on the tracks – were issued by the Apple label. Though these records did not achieve huge sales, and her contributions to concerts like London's Lyceum UNICEF benefit and Toronto's 'Rock 'n' Roll Revival' left most onlookers baffled, John was convinced of her influence on the 'new wave' of artists breaking through in the late seventies. He told Andy Peebles, 'I always think that some of

A *Two Virgins* album sleeve photo out-take

those kids at the UNICEF concert formed those freaky bands later. I hear touches of our early stuff in a lot of the punk, new wave stuff. I hear licks and flicks coming out. I'd love to know if they were in the audience ... because it sure as hell sounds like it.'

The partnership of John and Yoko represented a meeting of West and East, a Liverpool boy with a Tokyo girl, a rock and roll singer with a conceptual artist, a chauvinist with a feminist. Though the other differences were beyond her influence, Yoko succeeded in her efforts to alter John's opinion about women's place in society. She recalls that the breakthrough came with the discovery of a book by Elizabeth Gould Davies, *The First Sex*. 'It was advertised as a book to tell what women had done in history. John read it through the night, and when he finished it he was crying. It deeply affected him and he saw what men did to women.'

That revelation came in 1972 when John and Yoko were fraternising with the radical figures of New York's counterculture. His fervent new commitment to the feminist cause was expressed in a song that opened the Lennons' overtly political album *Some Time In New York City* and, in keeping with the tone of his 'newspaper songs' of this period, John found a hard-hitting slogan to hammer home the message. He reached back to an interview given to *Nova* magazine in 1969, and wrote a song based on Yoko's bold statement that 'Woman is the nigger of the world'. Including the line, 'If you don't believe me, take a look at the one you're with', John acknowledged that his song's sentiment was provoked by his own chauvinistic tendencies. 'I didn't realise what a pig I was,' he told his friend Elliot Mintz in April 1973, 'One doesn't realise until somebody tells you, and it's been hard for Yoko. It's been a slow process, 1973's

probably the final year ... I might be a whole human being by next year.'

Significantly, John spoke about the danger of being sidetracked from his transformation to a new man. 'Like in therapy, you hang on to your old habits because they're so internalised and programmed. But now, there's usually a warning light that goes on whenever I become that which I don't want to be.' Despite his optimism in that interview, the seeds of an imminent separation from Yoko had already been sown on an occasion when the warning light had failed to show.

In November 1972, John and Yoko had attended a party thrown by Jerry Rubin to watch the results of the presidential election on TV. It was a crushing blow when Richard Nixon won; it seemed that their campaigning had been in vain and that John was now less likely to overcome his problems with the Immigration and Naturalization Service. Yoko remembers, 'McGovern lost and John was drinking, and he was a little bit ... strange. There was a famous incident, actually, that John pulled another girl in the next room and they were "making it". So I thought this incredible outburst just means he wanted some freedom, couldn't say it, and expressed it in the most disastrous way imaginable.'

On John's album *Mind Games*, he sang 'Aisumasen (I'm Sorry)', a blues-tinged lament, apologising for his failings, 'When I hurt you and cause you pain, darling, I promise, I won't do it again. Aisumasen, Yoko'. But it was too late. By the time of its release, in November 1973, John was living in Los Angeles while Yoko remained in New York. It was the start of a sixteen-month separation that, for its first few months, was characterised by John's excessive drinking. Always adept at naming the different phases of his life, John dubbed this period his 'lost weekend', a reference to an Oscar-winning film starring Ray Milland as a dipsomaniac.

Certainly, John did hit the bottle hard but eventually he came to his senses, and when he returned to New York he was sober and productive, recording *Walls And Bridges* in just a few weeks. 'Production Co-ordinator' for the project was May Pang, John's constant companion throughout his separation from Yoko.

May had worked as John and Yoko's assistant since their film *Fly* in late 1970. When her employers' marriage foundered three years later, May states it was Yoko's wish that she and John should begin a relationship. 'Yoko said, "I know that John likes you". And I replied, "I don't want to go out with him." She said, "Oh yes you will", and that was how it all began.' Yoko does not acknowledge this story.

In October 1973 May Pang accompanied John to Los Angeles where recording began on the Phil Spector-produced *Rock 'n' Roll* album and where they were observed by Elliot Mintz. 'My point of view is that May was just one of a number of women that John had affairs with. A very attractive young lady, she did not smoke, drink or use any recreational pharmaceuticals. She was very much available, and perhaps supplied some kind of sexual relief for John's tensions. There was never anything between the two of them beyond that. May simply lacked the intellectual capacity that Yoko had to captivate the imagination of a man like John Lennon. I smile broadly at the concept that John and May would be a couple as John and Yoko would be a couple.'

The opinions of John's other friends in Los Angeles make Elliot's judgement seem rather harsh. 'John wasn't involved with other women as long as I was there. He really was very involved with May,' says producer Jack Douglas. 'But there was always the threat that he was going back with Yoko and he did miss her quite a bit.' Apple promotion executive Tony King agrees, 'They were having an affair, and it was obvious that John and May were close'. But he too was aware of the continuing power of Yoko in John's life, 'You could see that he was still incredibly connected to her. They couldn't live together and they couldn't live apart, but even though they were separated, Yoko would call up six times a day, so she still controlled the whole thing. She orchestrated the romance with May Pang.'

On *Walls And Bridges*, John wrote about the two women, and the songs are good pointers towards his feelings at the time. 'Bless You' is a languorous soul ballad for Yoko, tenderly expressing unselfishness, 'Whoever you are holding her now, be warm and kindhearted', and faith in their eternal bond, 'Remember although love is strange, now and forever our love will remain'. 'Surprise Surprise (Sweet Bird Of Paradox)', however, is a breezy, uplifting track for May, 'She gets me through this god-awful loneliness', in which John is taken unawares, 'Such a sweet surprise, I was blind, she blew my mind think that I love love love love her'.

Lennon's life with May was quite different from his life with Yoko. May was comfortable with rock musicians, encouraging him to meet friends like Mick Jagger, and to work with Elton John and David Bowie. Ten years younger than John, May draws a clear distinction between her role and Yoko's: 'I treated John as a boyfriend and lover, rather than somebody who wanted to run his life. I wasn't going to take over and tell him what to do, I wasn't going to be his mother.' But John was aware that he *did* need the maternal discipline and order that came from life with

Top Rehearsing in New York, August 1972

Bottom At Apple in November 1969

Yoko, whose solicitude was not unlike that of his Aunt Mimi.

Having returned to New York in April 1974 John and May lived in an apartment on the East Side of Manhattan. According to May Pang, John's reunion with Yoko in February 1975 was both sudden and unexpected, and she is convinced that his decision was affected by a hypnosis programme to quit smoking. He had long desired to give up cigarettes and agreed to undertake this cure at the Dakota apartment at Yoko's behest. May says: 'He told me it was like Primal Therapy. He said, "I kept throwing up because I became very weak". So it's hypnosis where, you know, ... the power of suggestion is very real ...' Yoko contends that, 'When we became separated I found John was keen on coming home. "Four days and I had enough," he said. From then on it was really a matter of convincing myself that I'm going to go back to that life where I'm hated by the world and I have no career opportunity and would be basically leading his life. But I was very touched [about] the way he felt about me and thought, "it's probably fate, we're going to get back together".'

Following their reunion the Lennons' lifestyle underwent a dramatic change. Tony King remembers that John had made plans for a new album. 'It was going to be called *Between The Lines* and be recorded with black musicians recruited by Carlos Alomar. Some songs were already written: one was for Tennessee Williams, called 'Tennessee Oh Tennessee', another was 'Nobody Told Me'. He was all keen to start, then I went round to the Dakota one day and John said, "Guess what? Yoko's pregnant!".'

The couple had suffered the sadness of three previous miscarriages during their hectic life in the late sixties, and now with Yoko aged forty-two, this seemed to be a last opportunity for them to have a child together. John devoted all his time to caring for his pregnant wife, and abandoned plans for recording the album. Following the birth of Sean Taro Ono Lennon on 9 October 1975, John retired from the music business and became a 'house-husband', looking after the baby and cooking the meals. Yoko took care of business at an office elsewhere in the Dakota building, completing the role-reversal of husband and wife. John told the BBC's Andy Peebles in 1980, 'I cannot do figures and numbers, she has the talent to do it. I had to contribute something, so I had the early relationship with Sean and it was fantastic! They did a real good skit on us on [the TV show] *Saturday Night Live*, with me in an apron and Yoko in a tie. We were hysterical, I don't mind the mickey being taken at all.'

John's feminist education was completed when he learnt how to cook and bake bread and participated in the care of his child. As he told Andy Peebles, such basic duties were an inspiration to him having previously been, 'just served by women, whether it was my Auntie Mimi or a girlfriend at college, who you'd expect to make the breakfast the next morning even though she'd been drunk as a dog too with you at the party. Suddenly, to get on the other side of the counter was quite an experience, and I appreciated what women had done for me all my life. I'd never even thought about it! That's how I feminised in a different way. As most housewives know, life becomes a routine between the meals. Okay, feed them ... you don't get a gold record, they just swallow it. If they swallow it, that means you're a hit.'

This new life left some of his old friends bewildered and feeling unwelcome. Mick Jagger was a next-door-neighbour in New York. 'I used to put messages under his door,' he says, 'but he was locked up by

Yoko. So obviously I resented that. She thought everyone from that [previous] life of his was someone that would turn him back into whatever she wanted to avoid him being.' In 1980, John gave his reaction to an *Observer* interview with Jagger, published during the 'house-husband' years. 'Mick said, "He's hiding behind Sean", and "Why doesn't he get his finger out. Yoko's got him locked up. Don't kid me that you're doing it for the family, because you can have both." Well he [Jagger] lived to learn *that* lesson because he didn't have both and that was before he split with Bianca and the child. It was more important [for me] to have a relationship with Yoko and the child.'

John returned to the music scene with *Double Fantasy* in November 1980, singing about this new experience of family life. 'Beautiful Boy (Darling Boy)' was unashamedly written to his son and 'Dear Yoko' was an unrestrained tribute to his wife, with echoes of 'Oh Yoko!' from *Imagine*. The album's mellow contentment and gentle optimism were at odds with many of the records released during the tail-end of 'new wave', but it found a huge audience when the tragedy of John's death shocked the world. In fact,

recognising that their generation had grown up with them, the Lennons were in the vanguard of the 1980s renaissance of 'mature' rock artists who avoided the traditional teenage subject matter of pop lyrics.

During their life together, John and Yoko gained a notoriety equal only to Richard Burton and Elizabeth Taylor, with whom they sometimes jokingly compared themselves. Their fame led millions to speculate about their relationship together, but during innumerable interviews John consistently affirmed the matchless impact of Yoko on his life. One of the last occasions was with *Playboy* writer David Sheff: 'Anybody who claims to have some interest in me as an individual artist, or even as part of the Beatles, has absolutely misunderstood everything I said if they can't see why I'm with Yoko. So for all you folks out there who think I'm having the wool pulled over my eyes . . . that's an insult to me! If you think you know me because of the music, and you think I'm being controlled like a dog on a leash because I do things with her, then screw you! You don't know what's happening. I'm not here for you. I'm here for me and her . . . and now for the baby.'

May Pang (right) in close conversation with Bianca
Jagger, while John talks to Ronnie Spector and US record
promotion man Pete Bennett in November 1974

'Woman, I can hardly express
My mixed emotions at my thoughtlessness
After all, I'm forever in your debt'

Mind Games

John Lennon's quest for inner contentment was a constant theme in his life, his songs charting his progress as he espoused, and then usually denounced, a mixed bag of substances and methods used to achieve peace of mind. His extraordinarily mature song 'There's A Place', recorded in 1963, showed an early fascination with self-discovery and the fulfilment such knowledge can bring. 'There's a place where I can go, when I feel low, When I feel blue. And it's my mind ...' Ten years later Lennon sang about 'Mind Games', in which 'the search for the Grail' was made in the knowledge that 'love is the answer'. His spiritual journey was tortuous and full of wrong turnings, but nevertheless one that he was compelled to make.

As a young musician, John turned to drink and then pills to pull him out of despondency and exhaustion. He and the other Beatles were introduced to pep-pills during long, strenuous nights onstage in the tough clubs of Hamburg. 'The only way to survive eight hours a night was to take pills,' he told *Rolling Stone* editor Jann Wenner in 1970. 'Pills and drink. I was a fucking drop-down drunk in art school, and I was a pill-addict until just

> *'The Beatles stopped touring and they had all the money and all the fame they wanted ... and they found out they had nothing. Then we started on our various trips of LSD and Maharishi. And the only way we got out of it was with* hope. *If we can sustain the hope then we don't need liquor, drugs or anything.'*
>
> JOHN LENNON

before *Help!*, when we turned on to pot and dropped drink. I've always needed a drug to survive.'

The meteoric rise of the Beatles in 1963 launched them into a hectic life of touring, recording and filming, in which the pressures that their colossal fame created were enormous. Working closely with them was record producer, George Martin, who was able to observe their conduct. 'It's tough for any young man to be subjected to those pressures without training. From my own experience, I know how much a man changes between the ages of eighteen and twenty-eight. Those ten years are incredibly formative and the Beatles all grew up and became mega-stars during that time. It really is amazing to me how they all coped with it so well and that they were, and still are, quite likeable people.'

Though the Beatles remained four friendly and approachable young men to the public, John candidly owned up to the hidden side of their fame in his 1970 interview with Jann Wenner. 'You have to be a bastard to make it ... and the Beatles were the biggest bastards on earth. All the hand-outs, the bribery, the police, all the hype ... everybody wanted in. You know, "Don't take 'Rome' from us, where

**October 1968: John and Yoko being ushered away from
Marylebone Magistrates Court where they were charged
with possession of cannabis resin. A later conviction led
indirectly to John's US deportation ordeal**

we can all have our houses and our cars and our lovers and our wives and office girls and parties and drink and drugs".' As the pampered Emperors at the centre of this contagion, the Beatles had easy access to drugs, which offered an escape route from the insanity surrounding them.

In a BBC interview in 1984, John's first wife Cynthia spoke about the welcome release that drugs had provided for him. 'John was so fascinated with anything extraordinary or unorthodox. He was such an open-minded man, he just tried them. I think that his ultimate high in life was when he stumbled across LSD. He realised the freedom [it gave] from the pain that he'd had as a child and was constantly battling.'

The hallucinogenic LSD, or 'acid' as it was usually known, entered the Beatles' lives in 1965. Legally available at the time, it was secretly slipped into their coffee at a dinner party hosted by a dentist friend of George Harrison. Stunned by its extreme mind-altering effects, John resisted the drug for a few months until it was proffered while the Beatles were staying at a house in Hollywood. The unnerving memory of Peter Fonda informing his fellow-trippers that he knew 'what it was like to be dead', provided the first line of John's song 'She Said She Said', released on *Revolver*. From then on, John later admitted, he 'used to eat it [LSD] all the time', partly for the hell of it and partly as a means of self-discovery.

John's music on *Revolver* reflected his experiences with the drug, musically and lyrically. He still retained his sense of humour though, lampooning a drug-peddling physician in New York with 'Dr Robert', 'Well, well, well you're feeling fine. Well, well, well he'll make you!'.

The Beatles' next album *Sgt Pepper's Lonely Hearts Club Band* was an equally acid-coloured creation and became the essential soundtrack for those who 'turned on' to the new drug culture of 1967. It was a relatively clear-headed recording however, except for one occasion when, by mistake, John took LSD in the studio. 'I thought I was taking some "uppers" and then it dawned on me I must have taken acid,' he later said. Recording engineer Geoff Emerick remembers, 'John suddenly looked up and said, "Cor, look at the stars, George", this was inside the control room and George Martin was looking around for these stars! Anyway, it was obvious that he wasn't very well so George took him for some fresh air on to the roof of Abbey Road – with no railings, no protection around it – and left him there. Of course, when he told Paul, George and Ringo what he'd done, they flew up the stairs to retrieve John because they could see that he was on a trip!'

LSD damaged John Lennon not only through the frequent, terrifying 'bad trips' it gave him, but also because its effects distorted his true personality. 'I got a message on acid that you should destroy your ego. And I did, I destroyed myself. I didn't believe I could do anything,' he told Jann Wenner. Fortunately for John, an alternative spiritual solution appeared just in time, when the Beatles met Maharishi Mahesh Yogi in August 1967.

It was through George Harrison's interest in Eastern music and religion that the Beatles were encouraged to learn about the benefits of the Maharishi's spiritual teachings. Holding forth to the BBC in 1967, the Maharishi explained that transcendental meditation would give people 'insight into life. They begin to enjoy all peace and happiness. Because this has been the message of all the saints in the past, they call me "saint".' Asked about the famous new converts attending his course at Bangor, North Wales, he described the Beatles as 'very intelligent

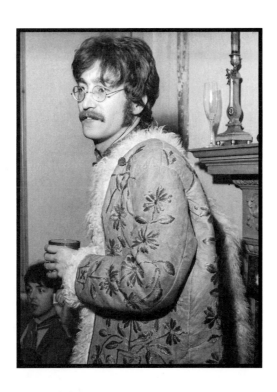

Top The acid-hued *Sgt Pepper* phase of
John's mind games
Bottom Happier times. George and John
flanking the Maharishi

and young men of very great potential in life ... they'll be the leaders for the next coming generation to spread this message of peace and harmony'.

Through his association with the Beatles, the Maharishi garnered inevitable worldwide publicity and was duly delighted when they travelled to his remote camp in Rishikesh, India for further study in February 1968. Meditating amid the peace of the Himalayas and forced to be alone with his thoughts, songs poured out of John Lennon. He wrote 'Dear Prudence' for Mia Farrow's sister, a child-like plea for her to take time off from her meditation and 'come out to play', and 'The Continuing Story of Bungalow Bill', a playful parody of a fellow camper. But the desperation of 'I'm So Tired' and 'Yer Blues' ('I feel so suicidal even hate my rock 'n' roll, wanna die') betrayed his deep-rooted inner turmoil.

After a few weeks, Paul and Ringo became bored by holy life in the hills ('a bit like Butlins,' Ringo said) and left early, but George and John's decision to leave was sparked by an alleged, scandalous incident. They were told that Mia Farrow had been propositioned in a less than spiritual manner by the Maharishi and, typically, John bluntly confronted him, saying they were leaving. 'He said, "Why?" ... and he gave me a look like "I'll kill you, you bastard!", because I'd called his bluff. I was a bit rough to him, I always expect too much. I'm always wanting my mother and don't get her,' he told Jann Wenner.

Feeling duped, John wrote a song about his feelings, substituting 'Sexy Sadie' for the word 'Maharishi' ('You made a fool of everyone'), and soon after his return home he plunged into a lifestyle dependent on LSD, cocaine and heroin. Keith Richards of the Rolling Stones remembers, 'John was on something for quite a while. That was the time when he used to come and visit me and he'd always end up throwing-up over the staircase. But I just thought he'd drunk too much. We'd never sit around and talk about "what you're on". I always thought that John was bigger than any drug that he took anyway.'

Even so, heroin was a devastating drug with which to do battle, and John's 1969 single 'Cold Turkey' graphically re-enacted the horrors of withdrawing from it. The stark musical atmosphere of the track was compounded by lines like 'I wish I was a baby. I wish I was dead', and a shocking two minutes of visceral screaming. It was another brutally honest message about his state of mind.

The chilling screams of 'Cold Turkey' presaged the next step John took in his search for a spiritual panacea. In April 1970, impressed by a book they had received called *The Primal Scream (Primal Therapy: The Cure For Neurosis)* John and Yoko contacted its author, American psychiatrist Arthur Janov, and embarked on a course of therapy. As discussed earlier, the possibility that his childhood trauma could be expunged proved overwhelming. Never one to tread cautiously, Lennon instantly believed he had found 'the answer'. Janov's wife, Vivian, also a therapist at the Primal Institute, comments, 'I think, maybe, he did go overboard. He thought, "Okay, the Maharishi disappointed me, now Janov is 'it'"", and I think Arthur may have represented the new brilliant father he never had.'

But as quickly as he could wholeheartedly embrace a new interest, Lennon could also drop it. After three months he suddenly cut short the course, returned to England and, although making a powerful record of his experience (the album *John Lennon/Plastic Ono Band*), never again had anything to do with the Janovs.

The next charismatic figures to

fascinate John with exciting ideas did so by practising the realities of political involvement rather than introspection. When the Lennons moved to the United States in September 1971, they swiftly became embroiled in the activities of noted New York radicals like Jerry Rubin and Abbie Hoffman. But again, despite initial earnest support, John withdrew from them almost overnight.

When his album *Mind Games* was released in November 1973, John reached another low point. As former Apple Records promotions executive Tony King recalls, 'He'd been booted out by Yoko, and he'd been through that political thing and been shamelessly used by a lot of those people. He looked incredibly sad at that time, and a bit damaged too.' John's reflex response was to blot out his misery by working hard in the studio and by drinking excessively. Unfortunately, he did the two things simultaneously.

John found an equally unhappy drinking buddy in Harry Nilsson, and while making an album together, they shared a beachside house in Santa Monica with Ringo Starr and Keith Moon, an equally volatile pair at this time. 'We were all so blitzed, when that group was together we were loaded all the time,' recalls Nilsson. A typical working day on his album *Pussy Cats* began in the studio at six in the evening then, continues Harry, 'Finish by 1 am, go back home, listen to the tapes, fall on the floor, bed by six'. John's 'lost weekend' label aptly describes this particular part of his separation from Yoko, and even the public became aware of his malaise when some drunken escapades hit the headlines.

One of the most infamous incidents occurred on 13 March 1974 when John and Harry Nilsson were forcibly ejected from the Troubadour club in Hollywood after their noisy outbursts interrupted the stage entertainment by American comedian-singers the Smothers Brothers. Almost a year later, John explained, 'That was the first night I had Brandy Alexanders [a deceptively potent mixture of brandy and cream] and I got drunk and shouted. It was a mistake but, hell, I'm human! I was drunk in Liverpool and smashed phone boxes but it didn't get in the papers then.'

Alcohol triggered an extreme personality change in Lennon, unleashing a violent aggression which was both destructive to himself and to others. He was a lousy drunk. Tony King witnessed some terrifying behaviour, the most reprehensible being one night following a Phil Spector session for *Rock 'n' Roll*. 'He was staying at [record producer] Lou Adler's house and Carole King's gold records got bent, walking sticks broken, windows smashed and Phil Spector had tied him up and left him on the ground. May Pang called me and I came over to the house, John was bellowing like a bull, he was actually frothing at the mouth. I had to wrestle and fight with him and hold him down. When he drank, he clicked back into some kind of maniacal personality that fed into all that drug abuse. When he crossed the line it was dangerous.'

In his 1980 interview with the BBC's Andy Peebles, John recognised the virulent reaction he had to alcohol. 'I don't drink now because it scares me, even a glass of wine knocks me out, so I'm happy about that. It was a pretty wild and miserable period and I'm thankful that I'm out of it. Forget about the booze.' His renunciation of drink came midway through the sessions for Nilsson's *Pussy Cats*. He returned to New York with May Pang and – for his own *Walls And Bridges* album – distilled his 'lost weekend' experience into the self-pitying ballad 'Nobody Loves You (When You're Down And Out)', in which, poignantly, he sang

---

Amid the disarray of the 'lost weekend'

**Brandy Alexanders are consumed with a vengeance
while John kisses May Pang, and Harry Nilsson squints
through the haze**

'Everybody loves you when you're six foot in the ground.'

Jimmy Iovine, who was in LA at the time as 'engineer-driver-coffee boy', has a clear understanding of one of the reasons why John allowed himself to 'cross the line'. 'He experimented. He pushed it. Sometimes it was a little dangerous but we wouldn't be talking about him now if he wasn't "interesting". He was *supposed* to push it, *supposed* to look in places that other people wouldn't look.'

Such behaviour took a heavy toll on Lennon, and after reuniting with Yoko in February 1975, they determined to lead a more centred life, free of artificial stimulants. Giving renewed attention to food, they adhered to a regime first adopted in 1969. Speaking at that time to Doug Pringle of CKGM–FM in Montreal John explained, 'We have a very strict macrobiotic diet, which makes you high as a kite, folks, with no paranoia ... well, very little! If you take as much trouble over your food as you do over your clothes, then you can find out where you can buy food that hasn't been touched by chemicals. I mean, there's enough brown rice for everyone and you can really groove on brown rice.'

If he occasionally 'fell off the wagon' in the 'house-husband' years, it seems his only vice was to eat a pizza or cheeseburger in the Hit Factory studio's maintenance room, while Yoko was not looking. As producer Jack Douglas remembers, 'John did look terrific. He was very thin and very muscular. He had been doing a lot of yoga and Yoko was really on this brown rice and sushi kick for them.'

On 27 July 1976, John was awarded his Green Card, finally winning his battle to remain in the USA. For the first time in nearly five years, he was free to travel outside the country secure in the knowledge that he would not be prevented from returning. This new liberty allowed the Lennon family to pay an extended visit to Japan, Yoko's home country, in June 1977. Here John was delighted by his temporary anonymity.

After 1976, Lennon was not contractually obliged to make new records and with his day-to-day loving care for Sean and his eye-opening trip to the East, he was experiencing a new and refreshingly different life. As a long-standing friend of both John and Yoko, Elliot Mintz has a special insight into John's spiritual well-being during the last few years. 'The road led back to what most would describe as something very conventional: family, a woman to love, a child to raise, a life spent together within the context of the family unit.'

Though this stability lacked some of the dizzy highs of the other stages along the rocky road, it also prevented the desperate lows that inevitably came with them. John remained curious about spirituality and had also cultivated an interest in the past. By John's bedside Mintz noticed books on the science of the mind, parapsychology, religion, and history. 'He also spent some time exploring his relationship with Jesus Christ and was impacted by fundamental Christianity. There was a particular television evangelist who affected him. He could not have reached that level of completion with family, had he not been touched by all the things that preceded it.'

Mick Jagger believes that John 'was always on the search for the pot of gold at the end of the rainbow, which seemed to alternate between a kind of asceticism, or a striving towards that, and bouts of hedonism, which in his case was just an excessive kind of lifestyle. But he did seem to be looking for something spiritual.'

John never lost his instinctive and courageous attitude to life. In July 1980, he and four-year-old Sean sailed down to

Bermuda and during a particularly ferocious storm, characteristically it was John, the novice sailor, who was prepared to take the wheel and steer the boat through the tumultuous sea. 'There were four of us on this 41-foot boat and it was the most fantastic experience I ever had, I loved it. I was buried under water, I was smashed in the face by waves for six solid hours, a couple of them had me on my knees. And I was having the time of my life, screaming sea-shanties and shouting at the gods!'

John Lennon was murdered outside the Dakota apartment building in New York by a deranged 'fan', Mark Chapman, on the night of 8 December 1980. It was the final, cruel twist of fate in a life that had threatened to self-destruct on previous occasions but had now found a secure axis. John had come out of retirement with *Double Fantasy* and was keen to release more albums and play concerts. He was a contented, loving husband and father. 'Life begins at forty' he joked in his last interviews. 'All right, so he lived only forty years which is half a lifetime, but he lived five lifetimes compared with what a lot of people do in theirs,' muses Tony King.

There can be no doubt of John Lennon's vibrancy, good humour, peace of mind and creativity at the time of his death. Today, hearing the tape of him talking to the BBC's Andy Peebles is a bitter-sweet experience, here was a man brimming with so much more to do and say. Recorded just two days before his death, John indicated just how happy he was. 'I've been walking the streets ... but it took me two years to unwind. I would be walking around tense, waiting for somebody to say something or jump on me. I can go right out this door now and go in a restaurant. You want to know how great that is? I mean, people come and ask for autographs or say "Hi", but they don't *bug* you ...'

'The road led back to something very conventional:
family, a woman to love, a child to raise ...'

JOHN LENNON INTERVIEWED BY ALAN FREEMAN

JANUARY 1975

During the last week of January 1975 John Lennon was interviewed by BBC Radio 1 disc-jockey Alan Freeman for one of his regular programmes. Freeman was in London, Lennon was in New York, and the interview was conducted by telephone.

This was a vital period for John. His last recorded album for five years, *Rock 'n' Roll*, was almost ready for release. He was still living with May Pang, yet within a fortnight would reunite with Yoko Ono at the Dakota and commence his lengthy 'house-husband' period following the birth of their son Sean in October.

Owing to problems with the telephone line, the interview was of poor technical quality and has never been broadcast. The following transcript is therefore the first public release of the interview in any form.

Alan Freeman: John, being in America at the moment, do you feel a sense of isolation at all?

John Lennon: Well, from what? Only from England, yes.

Alan: Do you think that it affects your music at all, this feeling of isolation from a country?

John: No, I don't think so, unless it's subliminal, you know. Because it's almost like in the old days, you know, one would write the music wherever one was, whether it was in Watford or Australia. So it was really how you were feeling. You weren't too conscious of where you were.

Alan: You don't feel that where you actually are is a necessary ingredient for the elevation of your songwriting?

John: No. I'm sure it affects it, but it's hard to put your finger on it. If I was not in America it might affect me more, but there's black music here for a kick off, which is my trip.

John: Do you feel that since the demise of the Beatles there's a very singular, lonely thing about yourself?

John: I think you can be lonely in a crowd as they say, right?

Alan: Very true.

John: But I guess it's the same as if you've been living with somebody and you don't live with them. Or especially if you've been living with somebody and you move in with somebody else. It's a bit different. But it's not a harmful experience inasmuch as most experiences aren't. There was definitely a gap there after working with or leaning on each other for so long. But it's a good experience to stand up on your own foot [sic], so I wouldn't have missed either experience. And only another ten years will tell me which was the more beneficial, in the end, to my creativity.

Alan: At this particular stage of your career, do you feel that you would prefer to be a songwriter in the singular, or do you feel that you would still like to really be writing with Paul McCartney?

John: Well I go through both feelings. I know Paul goes through this, because we were talking about it about a week ago, sometimes you get to a spot in a song where in the old days you would have said, 'Ah, I'll leave it here, I won't struggle with it. He'll fix it'. Right? It goes both ways, and we did a lot of writing on our own anyway, but there was always the feeling that somebody was there if you needed it.

Alan: Do you feel a greater sense of achievement, in fact, from having written a hit song by yourself, rather than having had any kind of inspiration from anybody else?

John: Actually, I thought I would feel more about it, you know, but it's not really that much of a bigger kick to just have one name on it. Still the kick is the creating of it, and then the manifestation of the creation on the record, and I think having had so much name-fame, that it's pretty hard to top what was already there you know, for whatever we did. So I can't say that I get that much big of a kick out of just seeing Lennon as being Lennon/McCartney, or Lennon/McCartney/Harrison/Starkey for that matter.

Alan: Do you think that had you not been a famous Beatle you would now get more satisfaction out of songwriting as a complete unknown, and starting from scratch again?

John: Well that's one of those questions, Alan. I just can't imagine it, you know. It's almost like saying 'If you hadn't been born' or something. I just can't visualise not having been what I am.

Alan: Do you think the Beatles revolutionised the world?

John: It sounds like a cliché, I've said it so many times, but I still believe that we were figureheads for what was happening anyway. We were like the ... what's that thing on the front of a boat?

Alan: The bow?

John: Yes, but they usually have a woman or a fish or something on the front, it was like we were that object, or we might have even been the guy up in the lookout tower, you know. But the whole ship was sailing along that way anyway, and because the person shouted 'Land Ho' everybody looked up at the top of the mast and said, 'Oh, that fellow discovered America'. But he just happened to be in the crow's nest. I really feel that. I'm not on a humble trip about 'Well, we didn't have any talent.' We had the talent to do what we had to do, but we could not have done that without the situation being what it was at the time.

Alan: Did you feel that your attitudes would influence the attitudes of people much older than you?

John: I don't think we were that conscious of it. We were more conscious of being the working-class, provincial lads who were going to show people what we could do. We did have part of an ear to the ground of the older generation inasmuch as we had an appreciation of music that came before the music we were making. I knew all about the music that the previous generation liked, and the generation before that, but we really were self-centred like most youth.

Alan: How is the single '#9 Dream' doing in America at the moment?

John: It's just gone into the Top 20. This coming week it's like 18, 17, that means it goes on the AM stations. You virtually have to be in the Top 20 to get played, and you get your initial exposure on the FM stations, which used to be called 'underground', which are really no longer 'underground' but they do play album tracks. So I've just broken through to the AM this week actually. I just heard that this morning, just before you called.

Alan: Why do you think that those 'underground' stations in America are no longer 'underground' and playing a lighter kind of music?

John: Well it was a nice explosion when it happened, but it did begin to get boring when you turned the FM on and all you got was either 'political rap' or twelve-hour guitar solos. So people just got bored with listening to it, and as the whole music scene always does, it goes round in cycles, and people have almost got back to wanting to hear two-minutes fifty-seconds of some good rhythm or a good melody.

Alan: I've always said that the fun period in pop music was from the birth of the Beatles until about 1968. I subsequently feel that perhaps we've had a little too much political social comment, and that it may have ruined a bit of the fun. It may have increased some of the great lyric writing, I think it may even have increased some of the great melody, but do you think that because of the political and social comment on pop records that a lot of the fun was lost?

John: Yeah, but I also happen to take some blame for that, because I got very involved in it myself. But it's no good crying over spilt milk. I think that whatever it was, that social awareness is now diluted into the music and it no longer stands out like a sore thumb. It's something that's there and has become part of the scene, it no longer dominates it, and I think that music, the way it seems to be going at the moment, seems to be getting back to that 'Let's have some fun' bit. It's like people's attitudes to social awareness as well. They are always talking about the students being apathetic. Now I don't know what they're saying about them in England at the moment, but it's not that they're apathetic, they're just a bit hipper than the mob, including ourselves, that were going round in the late sixties. So they're aware of what the scene is, but they know better than to just stick their thumb up somebody's nose. And I think

as that's been going on the music has also got a little gayer, if you'll excuse the expression, dear! The big scene over here, which is also happening there, is this disco music.

Alan: Tell us about that John, what's happening actually?

John: I know it's in your charts there too, the Disco Tex thing. But being of the age group that remembers the early sixties quite well, as far as I can see, the records are breaking in actual discotheques, like the old Ad Lib and the places in London. In the '63–'64 period we all listened to most of the early Motown stuff in all the discotheques. And a similar thing is happening here now. In fact, the music and the arrangements are not dissimilar to the early Motown period, but they're just a bit slicker because techniques have improved, etc etc. It seems like we're going through a recycle of the early sixties period, only with the improvements that the seventies have brought. I am not one of those that believes that rock and music and pop is dying, and that nothing good has happened since the Beatles or since Sinatra, or anything like that. I think the business is really alive. There's something in the air now, and it seems to be to do with early Motown.

Alan: That's very interesting to hear that. Can I move to another subject? Your appearance with Elton John at Madison Square Garden. I have never witnessed such an exciting night. I thought the crowd was at its zenith whilst Elton John was playing, and when you came on stage, after being announced by Elton, I honestly thought that the roof would physically lift off. What was your feeling about your reception, and about your performance in fact?

John: I was, as they say, very happy with

117

the reception. Because I haven't done it for a couple of years and one is always unsure of oneself going onstage, especially if you haven't been on for a bit. And of course I was thrilled with it. I think it's one of Elton's great assets that, being probably the biggest recording artist in the world at the moment, he doesn't need anybody or anything, and that he could share the spotlight with somebody else who is pretty well known themselves. It says something about Elton's personality, which I think is great. And the whole feeling of it, that he was setting it up and so worried that I would be comfortable and not regret it ... we all really enjoyed the experience. It was an emotional experience, and it's not something you can repeat.

Alan: I wondered exactly how you might be feeling when you closed the set with Elton, singing 'I Saw Her Standing There', and your jamming with Elton John and the fellas, that you never had the other three illustrious gentlemen around you. Did you feel anything strange about that?

John: Well it was double strange because I used to sing a third-part harmony underneath Paul on 'I Saw Her Standing There'. So I never actually sang the lead vocal. It was a really strange experience singing an early Beatle song that I never really sang, and singing it with somebody else. I was actually thinking, 'Oh, I wonder what Paul will think of this' (*laughs*).

Alan: I had an eerie feeling that Paul, George and Ringo might materialise out of nowhere, and even join you. I think that would have been possibly the most rapturous thing that could ever happen.

John: Well that means we've got something to come, right? (*laughs*)

Alan: Absolutely right, John. Can I ask you about the situation in America with yourself, and the latest developments on it, and what sort of hope we might have of seeing you here in Great Britain?

John: Well, to put it simply, the situation is the same as it was when they first started trying to throw me out. And it really came down from the old guard, the old administration, and it's like all government red tape. It seems that they started something that it might be embarrassing to stop, even if they want to stop they have to find a way to do it that makes them look all right. And whatever it is, it's a political decision. I'm in court, or my lawyer's in court. He goes from one court to the next, and they appeal, and then it's just like a normal court case, only it's about some abstract thing. And it's really down to somebody in Washington deciding, 'Oh you know, the guy's harmless, let him go'. Right? And my instinct is that it should probably happen this year, which means that they'll give me a bit of paper which would allow me to travel and come back when I want. I'm not the only one that has problems there – Mick, Keith, Paul, Paul's band ... Paul's supposed to be recording in New Orleans now, and he can't get Denny Laine in. And George has problems. We're all having problems constantly, but I sort of dug my heels in, and that made it more difficult for myself. It's probably something to do with my character, I don't know. But it's a matter of somebody giving me this Green Card, so that I can come and go as I want. And when they'll do it I really don't know, but I have a feeling it'll be sometime this year.

Alan: If you were, say this year of 1975, irrevocably told that under no circumstances could you get back to America if you left it, would you stay in America forever?

John: Well the thing is, I find it harder to answer speculative questions. That's almost the same as the one 'If you hadn't done that, what would you have been?' Until that situation arose I couldn't give you an answer. Being a Libra it's hard enough to make a decision on which piece of bread to eat, so to make a decision on forever like that, I couldn't do it, you know, and it just scares me even thinking about it.

Alan: What about this new album you've made with Phil Spector?

John: Ah well, as usual with me it seems that things are very complicated, Alan. I started the thing before *Walls And Bridges*, in '73 with Phil, and we went in and we cut half a dozen tracks over a period of eight weeks. So a lot of psychic phenomena, as I call it, was going down at the time. The album sort of ... the best word to use is 'collapsed' in the middle. Phil had a road accident, and I wasn't in exactly the highest state of mind at the time myself. And that is shown by the weird stories that were coming out of Los Angeles at the time. But we won't go into that! So between the two of us we collapsed. We cut a few tracks, then I went in, and did Harry Nilsson, to try and pull myself back together again. Then I went in and did my own album, *Walls And Bridges*, and then I went straight in and finished the oldies album by myself, meaning I didn't recall Phil again. By then there was such a sort of atmosphere about what we'd done before that I didn't feel like starting again with Phil. I almost started a brand new album. But just to make it simple, I ended up with half of the tracks that I cut with Phil, and half that I cut without him, and the album will probably go out sometime in March. Between that I did a few tracks with Ringo, and 'Lucy In The Sky' with Elton,

and I was doing all sorts. So I finally finished the *Rock 'n' Roll* album. I had the fun of not having written the stuff, not having thought about the lyric or the meaning, or trying to be a writer, which is what I really am, and I really enjoyed singing stuff that I sang when I was fifteen.

Alan: So you found real enjoyment interpreting other people's works?

John: Yes, it was almost like going back to my beginning, you know. I started out singing other people's songs, and this is like closing that circle. I've got it out of my system finally, of singing the stuff one always sings when the gang comes round and you pull out the guitars.

Alan: Finally John, do you have a message for your fans in Great Britain?

John: Yes, well it's a strange thing, a couple of them called this morning while I was asleep. I don't know how they got the number, and a friend of mine talked to them and they were saying, 'Well, tell him we miss him'. And I always get a little choked when I hear this, because I try not to feel emotional about not being able to come home, because then otherwise I would sort of back down from the fight I'm in, and I'm too stubborn to back down. I appreciate the letters that I get from England. I appreciate the people that buy my records or write to me, or think about me. I do think about them. I miss, you know, those English faces (*laughs*) and their voices, quite a lot sometimes. And I'm dying to come back, but being stubborn, I'll come back when I've won my war here. Maybe I can jump the space on TV which will be the next best thing. I'm talking about working on some TV projects here which would be shown in England too. That might do for now.

Alan: That'll be beautiful. John, thank

you very much for your time.

John: It was a pleasure, Alan. It was a pleasant surprise seeing you at Elton's concert too.

Alan: It was lovely being there. God bless you, John. Ta-ta.

John: Bye-bye.

COMPACT DISCOGRAPHY

The complete Beatles catalogue is essential listening and these fifteen CDs include every commercially available track recorded by the group:

Please Please Me
(Parlophone CDP 7 46435 2)

With The Beatles
(Parlophone CDP 7 46436 2)

A Hard Day's Night
(Parlophone CDP 7 46437 2)

Beatles For Sale
(Parlophone CDP 7 46438 2)

Help!
(Parlophone CDP 7 46439 2)

Rubber Soul
(Parlophone CDP 7 46440 2)

Revolver
(Parlophone CDP 7 46441 2)

Sgt Pepper's Lonely Hearts Club Band
(Parlophone CDP 7 46442 2)

The Beatles [the 'White Album']
(Parlophone CDP 7 46443 2)

Yellow Submarine
(Parlophone CDP 7 46445 2)

Abbey Road
(Parlophone CDP 7 46446 2)

Let It Be
(Parlophone CDP 7 46447 2)

Magical Mystery Tour
(Parlophone CDP 7 48062 2)

Past Masters: Volume One
(Parlophone CDP 7 90043 2)

Past Masters: Volume Two
(Parlophone CDP 7 90044 2)

To hear John Lennon's work outside the Beatles, there is a four-CD set including seventy-three tracks simply called *Lennon* (Parlophone CDS 7 95220 2)

The BBC Radio 1 FM series *In My Life: Lennon Remembered* was presented by Simon Mayo and broadcast on *Saturdays* at 1400, from 6 October to 8 December 1990; with repeat transmissions on *Tuesdays* at 2100, from 9 October to 11 December 1990.

The ten programmes covered the same subject matter as the chapters in this book and the following is a listing of all *Beatles* and *Lennon* related tracks heard in the series. If they are not featured on the CDs mentioned above, details are given:

PART 1: REMEMBER
'In My Life'
'Remember'
'Julia'
'My Mummy's Dead'
'I Found Out'
'Mother'
'You've Got To Hide Your Love Away'
'Cry Baby Cry'
'Ya Ya'[1]
'Cleanup Time'
'(Just Like) Starting Over'
'Beautiful Boy (Darling Boy)'
'Borrowed Time'
[1] *Walls And Bridges* (Parlophone CDP 7 46768 2)

PART 2: ROCK AND ROLL MUSIC
'Rock And Roll Music'
'Memphis, Tennessee'[2]
'Sweet Little Sixteen'[3]
'Too Much Monkey Business'[4]
'Some Other Guy'[5]
'Please Please Me'

'Twist And Shout'
'Dizzy Miss Lizzy'[6]
'Blue Suede Shoes'
'Well (Baby Please Don't Go)'
'Ain't That A Shame'
'Angel Baby'
'Just Because'

[2] *Decca Sessions 1.1.62* (Topline Records TOP CD 523)
[3] *1962 Live Recordings* (Baktabak CTAB 5001)
[4] BBC session (Broadcast in *Side By Side* 24.6.63)
[5] BBC session (Broadcast in *Easy Beat* 23.6.63)
[6] *The Beatles At The Hollywood Bowl* (Parlophone album EMTV 4)

PART 3: HELP!

'Help!'[7]
'She Loves You'
'Twist And Shout'[7]
'I Want To Hold Your Hand'
'It Won't Be Long'
'A Hard Day's Night'
'I'm A Loser'
'Ticket To Ride'
'Help!'
'Nowhere Man'
'And Your Bird Can Sing'
'I'm So Tired'
'Dig A Pony'
'Don't Let Me Down'
'God'

[7] *The Beatles At The Hollywood Bowl* (Parlophone album EMTV 4)

PART 4: IN HIS OWN WRITE AND DRAW

'Strawberry Fields Forever'
'Glass Onion'
'Working Class Hero'
'Ain't She Sweet'[8]
'I Want To Hold Your Hand'
'A Hard Day's Night'
'I Feel Fine'
'Yes It Is'
'You've Got To Hide Your Love Away'
'Lucy In The Sky With Diamonds'
'I Am The Walrus'

'Across The Universe'
'Happiness Is A Warm Gun'
'Love'

[8] *The Early Tapes* (Polydor 823 701–2)

PART 5: TOMORROW NEVER KNOWS

'Tomorrow Never Knows'
'Misery'
'In My Life'
'Rain'
'I'm Only Sleeping'
'Being For The Benefit Of Mr Kite!'
'Strawberry Fields Forever'
'I Am The Walrus'
'Two Virgins'[9]
'Revolution 9'
'Crippled Inside'
'#9 Dream'
'(Just Like) Starting Over'
'A Day In The Life'

[9] *Two Virgins* (Apple album SAPCOR 2) [Released as album Track 613012]

PART 6: TWO OF US

'Two Of Us'
'Twenty Flight Rock'[10] – *Paul McCartney*
'I Saw Her Standing There'
'Norwegian Wood (This Bird Has Flown)'
'Yesterday'
'We Can Work It Out'
'A Day In The Life'
'Revolution 1'
'I've Got A Feeling'
'Cambridge 1969'[11]
'The Continuing Story of Bungalow Bill'
'Too Many People'[12] – *Paul and Linda McCartney*
'How Do You Sleep'
'I Saw Her Standing There'
    with the Elton John Band
'Here Today'[13] – *Paul McCartney*

[10] *Choba B CCCP* ['The Russian album'] (Melodia A60 00415 006)
[11] *Unfinished Music No 2: Life With The Lions* (Zapple album ZAPPLE 01)
[12] *Ram* (Parlophone CDP 7 46612 2)
[13] *Tug Of War* (Parlophone CDP 7 46057 2)

PART 7: WITH A LITTLE HELP FROM MY FRIENDS

'With A Little Help From My Friends'
'Do You Want To Know A Secret'
'All Those Years Ago' [14] – *George Harrison*
'I'm The Greatest' [15] – *Ringo Starr*
'Slow Down'
'Baby's In Black'
'All I've Got To Do'
'Steel And Glass'
'Many Rivers To Cross' [16] – *Harry Nilsson*
'Old Dirt Road'
'Fame' [17] – *David Bowie*
'Lucy In The Sky With Diamonds' [18] – *Elton John*
'Whatever Gets You Thru The Night'
'Whatever Gets You Thru The Night' – *with the Elton John Band*

[14] *Best Of Dark Horse 1976–1989* (Dark Horse/Warner Bros 925726–2)
[15] *Blast From Your Past* (Parlophone CDP 7 46663 2)
[16] *Pussy Cats* (RCA album APL1–0570)
[17] *Young Americans* (RCA album RS 1006)
[18] *Greatest Hits Vol 2* (DJM album DJH 20520)

PART 8: GIVE PEACE A CHANCE

'Give Peace A Chance'
'The Word'
'All You Need Is Love'
'Revolution'
'The Ballad Of John And Yoko'
'Amsterdam' ['Stay In Bed For Peace'] [19]
'Instant Karma!'
'Come Together' [The Beatles' version]
'Working Class Hero'
'Power To The People'
'The Ballad Of New York City' [20] – *David Peel And The Lower East Side*
'New York City'
'John Sinclair'

'Scared'
'Imagine'

[19] *The Wedding Album* (Apple album SAPCOR 11)
[20] *The Pope Smokes Dope* (Apple album SW 3391)

PART 9: WOMAN

'Woman'
'You Can't Do That'
'If I Fell'
'Girl'
'I Want You (She's So Heavy)'
'John And Yoko' [21]
'Oh Yoko!'
'Woman Is The Nigger Of The World'
'Aisumasen (I'm Sorry)'
'Bless You'
'Surprise Surprise (Sweet Bird Of Paradox)'
'Dear Yoko'
'Nobody Told Me'
'I'm Stepping Out'
'Grow Old With Me'

[21] *The Wedding Album* (Apple album SAPCOR 11)

PART 10: MIND GAMES

'Mind Games'
'There's A Place'
'Dr Robert'
'She Said She Said'
'Lucy In The Sky With Diamonds'
'Dear Prudence'
'Sexy Sadie'
'Cold Turkey'
'Isolation'
'Nobody Loves You (When You're Down And Out)'
'Stand By Me'
'Beautiful Boy (Darling Boy)'
'Watching The Wheels'
'In My Life'

SELECTIVE BIBLIOGRAPHY

These books are worth seeking out for further study. Though long, the listing details only a fraction of the books published about the Beatles and/or John Lennon since 1963.

Unless otherwise stated, all books have been published in Great Britain, and the given publisher/date information is from the first British edition. Some titles have been subsequently updated and reprinted.

LENNON'S OWN WORKS

Lennon, John, *In His Own Write* (London: Jonathan Cape, 1964)

Lennon, John, *Skywriting By Word Of Mouth* (London: Pan, 1986)

Lennon, John, *A Spaniard In The Works* (London: Jonathan Cape, 1965)

John's own three books of prose, verse and drawings are essential reading. Published posthumously, Skywriting By Word Of Mouth *gathered together his hitherto unpublished writings and sketches.*

BEATLES, JOHN LENNON AND RELATED BIOGRAPHIES

Braun, Michael, *Love Me Do: The Beatles' Progress* (London: Penguin, 1964)

Coleman, Ray, *Brian Epstein: The Man Who Made The Beatles* (London: Viking, 1989)

Coleman, Ray, *John Winston Lennon, Volume One 1940–1966* (London: Sidgwick & Jackson, 1984)

Coleman, Ray, *John Ono Lennon, Volume Two 1967–1980* (London: Sidgwick & Jackson, 1984)

Connolly, Ray, *John Lennon 1940–1980* (London: Fontana, 1981)

Davies, Hunter, *The Beatles* (London: Heinemann, 1968)

Goldman, Albert, *The Lives Of John Lennon* (London: Bantam Press, 1988)

Hopkins, Jerry, *Yoko Ono* (London: Sidgwick & Jackson, 1987)

McCabe, Peter and Schonfield, Robert D, *Apple To The Core: The Unmaking Of The Beatles* (London: Martin Brian & O'Keeffe, 1972)

Norman, Philip, *Shout! The True Story Of The Beatles* (London: Elm Tree, 1981)

Tremlett, George, *The John Lennon Story* (London: Futura, 1976)

Wiener, Jon, *Come Together: John Lennon In His Time* (London: Faber, 1985)

Braun's was the first and, despite the limitation of being written only months into the group's period of fame, it remains arguably the best, though long out-of-print. Davies' is the only authorised Beatles' biography, though it was later denounced as sanitised by Lennon. Norman's is flawed but superbly written and is still the best Beatles biography on the shelves. Coleman's two Lennon volumes are solid, well-researched and were authorised by, in turn, John's first wife Cynthia and second wife Yoko. Goldman's is a dubious and entirely negative scandal-sheet, not for the faint-hearted. Wiener's book is an unsurpassable scholarly work, the only full account of Lennon's political and 'counter-culture' involvement. McCabe and Schonfield's work is the best available account of the Beatles' break-up.

LENNON INTERVIEW BOOKS

The Lennon Tapes – John Lennon and Yoko Ono In Conversation With Andy Peebles 6 December 1980 (London: BBC, 1981)

McCabe, Peter and Schonfield, Robert D, *John Lennon: For The Record* (London: Bantam, 1985)

Sheff, David (Golson, Barry G, ed), *The Playboy Interviews with John Lennon and Yoko Ono* (London: New English Library, 1982)

Wenner, Jann, ed, *Lennon Remembers – The Rolling Stone Interviews* (London: Penguin, 1973)

Three of these four make for essential reading. Lennon Remembers is the transcript of John's angriest ever interview, extremely revealing, bitter and full not only of first-time revelations about the Beatles but the choicest expletives known to man. Sheff's interviews took place over three weeks in September 1980; as one volume they represent the longest and most detailed interview Lennon ever gave. The Peebles book features the full transcript of John's last major interview, given to BBC Radio One just two days before his murder, and covers the post-Beatles period in especially good detail.

FIRST-HAND ACCOUNTS

Baird, Julia with Giuliano, Geoffrey, *John Lennon, My Brother* (London: Grafton, 1988)

Best, Pete and Doncaster, Patrick, *Beatle! The Pete Best Story* (London: Plexus, 1985)

Brown, Peter and Gaines, Steven, *The Love You Make: An Insider's Story Of The Beatles* (London: Macmillan, 1983)

DiLello, Richard, *The Longest Cocktail Party* (London: Charisma Books, 1973)

Epstein, Brian, *A Cellarful Of Noise* (London: Souvenir Press, 1964)

Fawcett, Anthony, *John Lennon: One Day At A Time* (London: New English Library, 1977)

Lennon, Cynthia, *A Twist Of Lennon* (London: Star, 1978)

Martin, George with Hornsby, Jeremy, *All You Need Is Ears* (London: Macmillan, 1979)

Pang, May and Edwards, Henry, *Loving John: The Untold Story* (London: Corgi, 1983)

Shotton, Pete and Schaffner, Nicholas, *John Lennon: In My Life* (London: Coronet, 1984)

Taylor, Alistair with Roberts, Martin, *Yesterday: The Beatles Remembered* (London: Sidgwick & Jackson, 1988)

Taylor, Derek, *As Time Goes By* (London: Davis-Poynter, 1973)

Taylor, Derek, *Fifty Years Adrift* (Guildford: Genesis Publications, 1984)

Williams, Allan and Marshall, William, *The Man Who Gave The Beatles Away* (London: Elm Tree, 1975)

Most are positive. Julia Baird was John's step-sister, Pete Shotton his schoolboy friend, Cynthia Lennon his first wife and May Pang his lover during the important 'lost weekend' period. Pete Best was the Beatles' original drummer, Allan Williams their first agent when still amateurs, Brian Epstein their first manager, Alistair Taylor his assistant and George Martin their record producer. Richard DiLello was the resident 'house-hippie' at Apple and Anthony Fawcett was John and Yoko's assistant during their remarkable 1968–70 'events' period. Derek Taylor, a writer second-to-

none, worked first for Brian Epstein then for Apple, was mentioned in 'Give Peace A Chance' and remains good friends with the ex-Beatles. However, though Peter Brown's credentials are almost as good – he too worked for Epstein and at Apple, and he too was mentioned in song by John Lennon – he opted to betray his friends in an ugly and often inaccurate portrait of their career.

PHOTOGRAPHIC BOOKS

Gruen, Bob, *Listen To These Pictures: Photographs Of John Lennon* (London: Sidgwick & Jackson, 1985)

Hoffmann, Dezo, *John Lennon* (London: Columbus Books, 1985)

Norman, Philip, *Days In The Life: John Lennon Remembered* (London: Century, 1990)

Ono, Yoko, ed, *John Lennon: Summer Of 1980* (London: Chatto & Windus, 1984)

Saimaru, Nishi F, *John Lennon: A Family Album* (London: Chronicle/Harrap, 1990)

Solt, Andrew and Egan, Sam, *Imagine: John Lennon* (London: Bloomsbury, 1988)

Hoffmann's photos of the Beatles mostly span 1962 to 1965, Gruen's book contains photos of Lennon from 1972 to 1980, Saimaru took exclusive photos of John, Yoko and the infant Sean during the 'house-husband' period. Of the others, Imagine: John Lennon *is a sumptuous coffee-table picture book issued to accompany the movie of the same name, Philip Norman's selection of agency photos is worth investigation and the text is typically well-written, and* Summer Of 1980 *contains an excellent selection of shots from John's last few months, compiled by Yoko from the collections of eight New York photographers.*

CRITICAL COMMENT

Cott, Jonathan and Doudna, Christine, eds, *The Ballad Of John and Yoko* (London: Michael Joseph, 1982)

Sauceda, Dr James, *The Literary Lennon: A Comedy Of Letters* (Ann Arbor: Pierian Press, 1983)

Thomson, Elizabeth and Gutman, David, eds, *The Lennon Companion: Twenty-Five Years Of Comment* (London: Macmillan Press, 1987)

Cott and Doudna's book is a very readable collection of articles and interviews for Rolling Stone, *Thomson and Gutman's is an intelligent collection from a great many diverse sources, Sauceda's book is a critical study of Lennon poetry and prose but regrettably written three years before Yoko revealed a hitherto unknown collection, the posthumous* Skywriting By Word of Mouth *volume.*

MISCELLANEOUS/INFORMATION BOOKS

Baker, Glenn A, *The Beatles Down Under: The 1964 Australia & New Zealand Tour* (Glebe, Australia: Wild & Woolley, 1982)

Carr, Roy and Tyler, Tony, *The Beatles: An Illustrated Record* (London: New English Library, 1975)

Castleman, Harry and Podrazik, Wally, *All Together Now* (Ann Arbor: Pierian Press, 1975)

Castleman, Harry and Podrazik, Wally, *The Beatles Again?* (Ann Arbor: Pierian Press, 1977)

Castleman, Harry and Podrazik, Wally, *The End Of The Beatles?* (Ann Arbor: Pierian Press, 1985)

Dowlding, William J, *Beatlesongs* (New York: Simon & Schuster, 1989)

Evans, Mike, *The Art Of The Beatles* (London: Anthony Blond, 1984)

Harry, Bill, *The Book Of Lennon* (London: Aurum Press, 1984)

Harry, Bill, *Mersey Beat: The Beginnings Of The Beatles* (London: Omnibus Press, 1977)

Howlett, Kevin, *The Beatles At The Beeb: The Story Of Their Radio Career, 1962–1965* (London: BBC, 1982)

Lewisohn, Mark, *The Beatles Live!* (London: Pavilion Books, 1986)

Lewisohn, Mark, *The Beatles: 25 Years In The Life* (London: Sidgwick & Jackson, 1987)

Lewisohn, Mark, *The Complete Beatles Recording Sessions: The Official Story Of The Abbey Road Years* (London: Hamlyn, 1988)

Miles, ed, *John Lennon In His Own Words* (London: Omnibus Press, 1981)

Ono, Yoko, *Grapefruit* (London: Peter Owen, 1970)

Robertson, John, *The Art & Music Of John Lennon* (London: Omnibus Press, 1990)

Stannard, Neville, *The Beatles: The Long & Winding Road – A History Of The Beatles On Record* (London: Virgin, 1982)

Stannard, Neville and Tobler, John, *Working Class Heroes – The History Of The Beatles' Solo Recordings* (London: Virgin, 1983)

A small selection from a great many books in this category, mostly factually-based reference works – lists, discographies, a study of recordings, chronologies, accounts of tours, record reviews, artworks, quotes and critiques. Outside of all these categories is Yoko's Grapefruit, *unusual and entertaining, to say the least.*

INDEX